MACMILLAN
HEINEMANN
English Language Teaching

BROOKLANDS COLLEGE LIBRARY
WEYBRIDGE, SURREY KT13 8TT

Macmillan Heinemann English Language Teaching Oxford
A division of Macmillan Publishers Limited
Companies and representatives throughout the world

ISBN 0 435 24060 9

© Michael Lewis and Jimmie Hill 1993
Heinemann is a registered trademark of Reed Educational and Professional Publishing Limited

Acknowledgements
The Authors and Publishers would like to thank the following
for permission to use material: W Foulsham and Co. Ltd for
an extract from *Solve a Crime* by A C Gordon; Longman Ltd
for an idea from *Teaching English as a Second Language* by
J A Bright and P G McGregor; Peter Naylor; All the former
assistants who sent in lesson ideas for this new edition;
Anthony Howick, Head of Assistants Department at The
Central Bureau for Educational Visits and Exchanges, for
his invaluable advice.

Printed and bound in Great Britain by
The Bath Press, Bath

98 99 00 01 02 03 12 11 10 9 8 7 6

Contents

Introduction: *A year abroad*

The Source Book for Teaching English Overseas was used by many teachers working in schools in many different countries. When we prepared this successor, we asked many who had used our original *Source Book* for their comments. Here are some of the most useful points that language assistants wished to emphasise. We were encouraged by the fact that these were points we had emphasised before. You can feel confident that the advice offered in this book is tried, tested and endorsed by your returning colleagues!

'I found widespread apathy among students about social issues.'
'It took me a long time to realise the truth of the advice that *it can never be too simple.*'
'You don't realise how much power you have just by being a native-speaker.'
'Speak English whatever happens.'
'Speak English whatever happens.'
'Speak English whatever happens.'
'You are not a defender of everything your country has ever done – just a person with your own individual opinions.'
'My main value was in giving students the chance to speak English without being constantly corrected. They were surprised I was interested in what they had to say.'
'Advice? Easy. Grab 'em immediately, look at 'em constantly, really listen to 'em, make it fun for 'em – and finally, remember you will never meet each other again after the end of the year.'
'What you get out is proportionate to what you put in.'
'However good they are, it's always best to have something concrete to base the lesson on.'

Some of the most successful lessons described to us by former assistants are outlined in Chapter 14.

So you are going to spend next year abroad, teaching your own language. For you, the teaching part of the year may seem more or less incidental. The main emphasis for you may be on learning your host's language, and the stimulation of living in an interesting and unusual environment.

It may well be that the last thing you intend to be later in life is a language teacher, but for the next twelve months at least, language teaching is going to form a significant part of your life. Many people have memories of meeting a foreign language assistant at school themselves: dreary 'conversations' initiated by a rather limp request 'What would you like to talk about?' Horror of horrors – have you really chosen to do that? To subject others to what you were subjected to yourself? But, done well, working as a foreign language assistant can be rewarding, fun and valuable to all concerned.

The experience of working as an assistant teacher can be very different in different countries, or even in different schools. Some assistants have small groups, others have complete classes; some have only older or more able students, while others have youngsters of only twelve or thirteen years old whose English is poor; some are in schools with good facilities and helpful staff, while others are not so lucky. Be prepared to adapt to your situation and try to swim with, rather than against, the tide. If your school or college has strong ideas about what you should do, try to do your best to follow those requests or suggestions. In many cases, however, the school will either be quite happy to leave it to you, or will make only the most general suggestions: 'Talk to them.' Or, even worse, 'Get them to talk.' In this book we give a range of activities and materials – many of them photocopiable – that provide you with almost instant lessons. You will be able to use these to make those conversation lessons more useful and more fun than the classes that you may well remember from your own school-days.

Your year abroad offers both your students and yourself an invaluable experience, provided what happens in the classroom is taken seriously. It does not mean hours of preparation, but a little thoughtful careful reading when you first start, and then a willingness to prepare and select materials, and above all to think how you are going to use them in class. Time spent thinking about the class beforehand will generally be repaid. Forty-five or sixty minutes in front of a group of people who do not want to be there, doing something which you have not planned and which you can feel all too clearly is not working, has a negative effect which can easily spill over into your life outside the classroom. Put a little effort into preparation – of yourself and your materials – and the whole of your stay will be more successful, more relaxing and more rewarding.

One of the main themes of this book is that your conversation lessons should be both of those things – conversations and lessons. If you only attempt to get the students to talk, both they and you will end up frustrated. A little more formal teaching – pronunciation practice, a vocabulary– building exercise etc. – will give a structure and direction to everything you do, and, because of your more positive attitude and approach, will be more likely to make the conversation aspect more successful as well.

A most important piece of advice: use only English in your lessons. This may be seen to be making things artificially difficult for yourself, but nothing could be further from the truth. There are distinct advantages to using only English. Firstly, you will be competent in your use of it, and express yourself more fluently and accurately than you will in any other language. Secondly, if there is a misunderstanding, it will be because the students misunderstand, not because you have not said what you meant. Thirdly, people's comprehension of a foreign language is always greater than their ability to use it. Clear, simple English is more likely to keep you out of trouble than mistake-ridden German, for example. From a disciplinary point of view it is extremely important to avoid any form of confrontation. If a student says something impertinent in their own language which you hear, and which they know you have understood, you will be obliged to react. If you can keep a straight face and simply say, 'I'm afraid I don't understand. What does that mean?' Very few people, in our experience, are prepared to repeat something impertinent directly to you – particularly if you are smiling encouragingly at the time. Finally, all the time that you are speaking English to the students, you are providing them with good language practice. The primary way we learn a language is through listening. One of the reasons your knowledge of their language will improve while you are abroad is because of the enormous amount of time you will spend listening. Even if you are not responding or taking any overt part in a conversation, you will benefit from the language you hear casually on the radio, while washing your clothes, while travelling on public transport etc. Every bit of English you use in class – providing you try to keep it simple and within the student's range – will be of direct help to them.

For many years we lectured to people who were going abroad in the way that you are now planning to go abroad. Many provided feedback when they returned to Britain. The most common comment of all was 'Why didn't you stress more firmly that I shouldn't use the students' language?' We always insisted and stressed this point, but remember in a single moment you can give the game away by using the students language just once. Don't! When you arrive you have an in-built advantage – you are a novelty, the 'real thing', and you speak English naturally. Don't throw away that advantage by using the students' language in your classroom.

Sometimes you may have the feeling that you are being asked to be both more and less than yourself: a British student working in a foreign school can be asked not to be themselves, but to be the representative of all things British. This is an unreasonable, but not uncommon, request. It is important to resist the temptation to pontificate on your own country. As we explain in detail later, we suggest you do not generalise, but seek always to personalise. Offer the students *your* experience, *your* opinions without pretending that they are 'typical' of anything.

A year abroad can be infinitely rewarding, and the teaching part of that year can contribute greatly to either the success or failure of the whole year. Don't go with the idea that you are going to change the world, but do go with the idea that you are going to make a real, and valuable contribution. Try to prepare your work so that it will be of real benefit to your students. If you do this, you will discover that the whole experience benefits you.

We very much hope this book will help you to get as much as possible out of the experience of the coming months.

– *Michael Lewis, Jimmie Hill, Hove, 1993.*

Chapter 1   Before you leave home

Before you get to the place which will be your home for the next year, the classes you are going to take probably seem rather remote. But remember that while you are at home and before you go, you are surrounded by English language materials and a host of ordinary things which will make your lessons easier for you and more interesting and concrete for the students. So it is worth giving some thought, while you still have the chance to do something about it, to the sort of things you may either need, or at least find useful, while you are out there.

Information about home

Apart from the personal things you take, it will probably be a good idea to take a number of copies of the sort of free official information which you can easily get from information offices, railway stations, post offices, travel agents, theatres and so on. If you do take such things, take enough of them so that students can have one each, or make sure they are large enough if you're going to have a group of students looking at them. Remember, too, that you will need spare copies for those that get damaged or lost.

The following may be useful:
- Pocket timetables from your local railway station.
- Copies of railway brochures about what kind of ticket you need.
- Pocket maps of the underground or subway (available from the information bureaus in most of the bigger underground stations). Alternatively, a large map of the underground/subway system.
- Maps of the capital city of your country. You can usually obtain these free from the Tourist Board.
- Brochures advertising guided tours – either of the city, or a town near where you live, or even an area of the country near where you live. If you live in a tourist town it's usually possible to get a *What's On* brochure or card which is displayed in local shops. You will find that materials you have found which students will see as the 'real thing' are better than anything which you can take from any book. In addition to the *What's On* guide suggested above, several different copies of the entertainment guide from your local newspaper can be a good idea. Local papers are usually better than the national papers for this as they have a wider range in a smaller area of paper than, for example, the theatre guide in the national press. Remember, too, that the latter will probably be rather outside the experience of most of your students and the page from the local paper with cinemas, discos, clubs, and so on will probably be more practical. In the same way, it can be a good idea to take several pages from the paper listing the evening's or weekend's television programmes.

- Information about the opening times and facilities of any local attraction near where you live – a country house, a zoo, a museum, or whatever. It is not particularly important when choosing this information that the place is one that your students might want to visit. You use it as a concrete basis for situations.
- Several maps of the town and/or brochures about local services from any tourist town near where you live.
- A store guide from any large department store.
- A poster or guide for foreign visitors on how to use a local telephone.
- A few pub or café menus. One of the main problems people face when they go abroad is feeding themselves, and often their most immediate problem is understanding a menu – particularly a pub lunch or snack bar menu. The whole thing will be much more realistic if you are prepared to write out the menu yourself on cards. Most pubs have these supplied to them and a request at your local will probably get you half a dozen blank cards.

Information about your host country

Students are very often interested in information about their own country – particularly if it's inaccurate! While you are at home you will find it easier to get English language material about the country you will be going to. There are four sources:

- The Tourist Office or Consulate. Write and ask for any information they have in English about the part of the country you are going to.
- Your local travel agent. Here you should find a number of brochures advertising trips to different parts of your host country. Most of them will have little descriptions of the area with the main attractions mentioned.
- Most books used in schools now for teaching French for example, have some information about France. If you have a younger brother or sister who is using a textbook, take copies of the pages that give information about 'Marcel's typical day at school' or other pieces of information which purport to represent typical French life. You can use these even if they are in French – the students can then tell you whether the French is correct or not and whether the information contained in the book is correct or not. In most cases that should stimulate comment!
- Keep your eye on newspapers for articles and news items about your host country. Short news items are more useful than long, thoughtful, analytical articles. The ideal is the short news item which displays a clear prejudice about the host country. Avoid ones that are particularly topical and will therefore seem dated if used in six months' time. If anything of particular interest happens in the country you're going to visit in the months before you go there, it's worth buying several newspapers – a variety of quality papers and the more popular press – and taking out different articles about the same incident, topic or personality.

Books and magazines

It would be easy to give a long list of books which may be of use, but we have tried to avoid that. The policy we have employed here is to *exclude* as many books as possible. Most of you will find that the school has an extensive library of basic textbooks, dictionaries and grammar books. To be realistic, you will not want to spend a lot of money taking books which may not be useful. Read the notes we have added to the various books here, think in advance of the age and level of your students, and try to take only those things that you really will use. Most of the books recommended will be difficult to get when you are actually in the host country. A small investment before you go will save you many hours of worry preparing classes.

Reference
Practical English Usage, Michael Swan, OUP.
Worth having your own copy even if it is available in the school library.
The best of its kind. Indispensable.

An A to Z of British Life, Adrian Room, OUP.
Alphabetically arranged explanations of 3000 aspects of life in Britain.
Do you know how many seats there are in the House of Commons?

Games
Play Games with English Teacher's Resource Book, Colin Granger, Heinemann.
Three graded books at beginner, elementary and intermediate levels.
Word Games with English, Deirdre Howard-Williams and Cynthia Herd, Heinemann.
A series of graded books of games and puzzles for building vocabulary.

Word Games with English Plus, Deirdre Howard-Williams and Cynthia Herd, Heinemann.
Similar to above but more difficult.

Elementary/Intermediate/Advanced Communications Games, Hadfield, Nelson.
Three books of photocopiable materials, classics of their kind.

Grammar
Grammar Games, Mario Rinvolucri, OUP.
Not really games, but a wonderful resource book if you are interested in practising more specific language points.

Of the plethora of student's grammar practice books on the market we are happy to recommend:
COBUILD Students Grammar, COBUILD.
Grammar and Practice, Hill, LTP.

You will find all the grammar reference you need in Michael Swan's *Practical English Usage* (above).

Dictionary
COBUILD Essential English Dictionary, COBUILD (In Germany this dictionary is called *PONS/COBUILD*).
What makes this dictionary different is the defining style which teaches you how to explain in class – it explains by giving an example rather than a definition.

Miscellaneous
Magazines: You may find that your school subscribes to ELT magazines. The best known are published by Mary Glasgow and contain lots of highly practical lesson material.

Team teaching
If you are an assistant in Austria or on the JET scheme in Japan, you may find yourself working very closely indeed with your host colleagues. In those circumstances we recommend *Team Teaching*, Sheila Brumby and Minoru Wada, Longman.

Finally, may we modestly recommend *Practical Techniques for Language Teaching*, Michael Lewis and Jimmie Hill, LTP.
Like the present work, it is highly practical, covering basic classroom technique in a comprehensive way for the new teacher.

Your own tape

You may have a cassette tape recorder and are thinking of taking it with you for your year abroad. If so, a few short tapes prepared in advance while you are still at home will provide variety and extra interest for your lessons. Here are a few ideas for things you could record:
- Four or five different native-speakers from different parts of the country who have distinguishable accents yet still speak clearly. You could also add one person who has a much stronger accent.
- One or two older people talking about how things have changed.
- With two or three friends record some short (6–9 line) dialogues which illustrate the language mentioned in Chapter 5. You will find these dialogues most natural if you record them using an outline script, but allow the people who are speaking on the tape to deviate slightly from the script if they find it more natural to add a word, take a word away, pause or whatever. Make sure before you use them in class that you are certain of the exact words that are used on the tape.
- Perhaps the most effective of all recorded materials is if you interview people who have lived in your host country. You should ask them to express one or two views which are decisive enough to prompt correction or opposition from the class. The ideal people to interview for this purpose are probably people who have spent a year as an assistant and therefore have some idea of how difficult the language they use can be, so that the interviews are difficult enough to keep students interested but easy enough

not to be outside their range. If you are going to teach older, more capable students, a short recording of three or four people discussing their attitudes to the host country or any other question for that matter can be helpful. It is, however, very difficult for students to follow a discussion with three or four native-speakers speaking naturally together, so you should only use this for those in the last years of school when you are sure that it will not be beyond them.

Any tape you make should be short, or at least easily divisible into short (2–5 minute) sections. Listening to a tape of a native-speaker can be very difficult indeed and you must never use more than a few minutes of tape in any lesson. A couple of hours spent with some friends who are also going abroad preparing a tape will probably save you a lot of evenings trying to dream up something to do once you get out to your host country.

Miscellaneous materials

The items that follow do not fit into any particular pattern but are all things which are easy to obtain before you leave and which make it much easier to teach one or more lessons from the concrete plans suggested later.

- A plastic outline stencil of your host country (these are normally available very cheaply from stationers).
- Two or three greetings cards – for example, a Valentine card.
- Several pictures that are typical of your country – if you keep your eye on the colour supplements and other magazines you will find pictures which are unmistakably 'home' to you.
- Any questionnaires that appear in magazines.
- One or two books of language puzzles (but not crosswords). Particularly if you're going to teach younger children you will find that these books provide a source of material and, perhaps above all, a source of ideas for the kind of language games you can make up yourself. The most likely place to find such books is in the children's department of any good bookshop.
- A small number of teenage magazines aimed at the age group you're going to teach, or at an age group that is slightly younger than the one you are going to teach. (Remember, there will be a language problem.)
- Any short letters to the press which express strong views about topics you think will be within the capabilities of the age group you're going to teach. Again, if it's a real letter out of the newspaper it provides a more concrete basis for discussion than something you merely make up.
- Pictures of well-known people.

Summary

There are three things you can do before you leave which will ensure that you enjoy your time abroad and be more effective, both in your classes and in your own learning of your target language:

1 **Listen** to ordinary people using English, particularly acquaintances and strangers. Try to get some feel for what does sound natural and what does not. Do not concern yourself with studying the grammar, but rather try to make sure that you can guide your students accurately towards the sort of language that they should use in everyday situations.

2 **Collect** the various materials listed above, bearing in mind that only a selection of them will be suitable for the particular age level that you are going to teach.

3 **Think** about what you're going to do in some of your first classes. Do not wait until you get out to the host country and then start to worry. Plan a few lessons before you leave. You may change your mind completely once you get abroad, but at least you will have thought some things out, and if you need any special materials you will have taken them with you. The more concrete your preparation, the more effective it's likely to be and the more relaxed and effective you are likely to be.

Chapter 2   Being an assistant

What to expect

Co-operation works best when both parties involved have the same, or at least similar, expectations. So what can an assistant expect from the host school? And what can the staff, students, and system of the receiving school expect from someone who is untrained as a teacher, and as concerned with improving their French, Spanish or German as with helping the students with their English?

Your expectations

Some assistants have a wonderful time – socially, academically, linguistically, and in every other way. Some schools receive assistants warmly, are well-organised and have a clear plan for what they would like the assistant to do. But this will not always be the case. Realistically, you are a 'blip' on the normal life of your host school. You are there briefly, a possible help, but maybe equally a mild inconvenience. The previous assistant may have been dynamic, and integrated into the life of the school, and popular. Or she or he may have been work-shy and unhelpful. The students may be keen, well-motivated, and speak English well. If so, count your blessings, for you have met one of the small group of the minority. Much more likely, you will meet a group of less-than-well-motivated students, shy, anxious about speaking English, and perhaps used to being bored by last year's assistant. Frequently, your promised timetable may not materialise, or the small group you expected could turn into a whole class. The message is simple – try to keep your expectations realistic. Experience of returning assistants reveals that many are virtually ignored by most of the staff of their school, including the English teachers. Be pragmatic and try to ensure that you can benefit from, and perhaps even positively enjoy, the situations with which you are confronted!

Your host's expectations

What will be expected of you as an assistant? Host schools, and host teachers, vary enormously. Not all will be well organised! Some will place considerable demands upon you; others leave you largely to your own devices. No one can say what your particular situation will be. It is possible, however, to give a few guidelines.

Nowadays most schools believe that they are teaching communicatively. Nominally at least, students are expected to understand and speak English, and only at a comparatively advanced level to be able to write English. In practice, however, grammatical syllabuses and grammar teaching continue to dominate many school systems, particularly with older, more conservative or traditional teachers. Teachers in most state schools will talk easily about *the second conditional, the passive*, and *wh- questions*, and be surprised if you are not familiar with this terminology. If you are not, you may like to have access to a good grammar of English as a foreign language. There may be one in the library of your school, but taking one with you is the only way of being sure that you have a reference for yourself.

Most teachers will now be using a textbook which, in addition to language structures, also makes frequent reference to language functions – inviting people, offering, refusing and such-like. Teachers may be surprised if you are not familiar with this terminology, and the language which is associated with it. Here, the best way to provide yourself with a resource is to obtain a copy of the student's textbook. Before reading the textbook, look first at the contents page which in many cases will list both the structures and functions dealt with in each unit. If the language or the terminology seems new, familiarise yourself with it.

In addition to language study, in many countries the study of British life is part of the student's course. The content of these courses varies greatly from country to country. It may involve literature (particularly in Italy), the British 'system' and detailed factual information, and even the trivia of British life such as pubs, fish and chips and the like. Sometimes you may be surprised by the content of textbooks, or even teachers' individual ideas on this kind of topic – they may be stereotyped, and out of date. Rather than bringing yourself into conflict with the teachers, the advice offered in our Golden Rules in Chapter 3 is relevant – *don't generalise, personalise*. By talking about your experience, and confining yourself to comments of a personal type, you can make yourself more interesting to the students, and avoid arguments with host colleagues.

Teaching methods

Different countries have very different expectations for what constitutes a normal class. In addition to this, your own expectations will be very different depending on whether you come from a traditional, more academic school or one with a more liberal approach. Some schools will only be familiar with a teaching mode which involves the teacher at the front of the room addressing the whole class. In such schools silence from the participating class may well be normal. If you expect to interact or converse with the class, you are in some ways a challenge to the whole system. In other schools, students breaking into groups and working independently will be common. If you try to impose yourself on the whole class you may be going against class and colleague expectations. Very little advice can be given on how to counteract this, except to say be sensitive to the situation. If you find that what you do meets with incomprehension, before ploughing on, try to consult colleagues and see whether you have broken the norms of expected behaviour either for the class, the host teacher, or even the whole host culture. When expectations coincide, a good atmosphere and success are around the corner. Try, as far as possible, to make your expectations realistic and talk to your host colleagues or head of department about their expectations before you go into class. It won't always be easy, but it will almost always be worth the effort.

Teaching your own language

As a native-speaker of English, unless you have done some English as a foreign language (EFL) teaching before, you will not have had cause to think of your language from a learner's point of view. It will be comparatively easy for you to say what is, and is not possible in English, but more difficult for you to say what people actually say, rather than what they could say, and very difficult indeed for you to say why they say what they say – why particular expressions are possible, while others are not. Some of the explanations will be obvious to your students, and certainly to your host colleagues. Here is a list of questions about the English language which a student may ask. Don't worry if you can't answer them, but do at least reflect that setting out to teach your own language is a serious task, which can be intellectually challenging as well as any other challenge it may present.

a) It seems as if 'I have to be there by 8 o'clock.' and 'I must be there by 8 o'clock.' mean more or less the same thing, so why is there a difference between 'I mustn't be there by 8 o'clock.' and 'I don't have to be there by 8 o'clock.'?

b) Why can you say 'They have a wonderful climate in Spain.', but you can't say 'They have a wonderful weather in Spain.'?

c) What is the difference between 'I speak German.', 'I am speaking German.', and 'I can speak German.'?

d) What is the difference between 'journey' and 'trip'? Which should I say when my friend is going to the Canaries for a week – 'Have a good journey.' or 'Have a good trip.'?

e) You can say 'She is very interesting.' or 'She is a very interesting girl.', and you can say 'She's asleep.', but you can't say 'She's an asleep girl.' Why not?

f) What is the difference between 'I saw him during the weekend'. and 'I saw him at the weekend'.?

g) Is there any difference between 'Excuse me, does this bus go to Victoria?' and 'Excuse me, is this bus going to Victoria?'?

h) What is the difference in meaning between 'I'll tell him if I see him.' and 'I'd tell him if I saw him.'?

Most of the above are standard questions about English as a foreign language. If working as an assistant is your first contact with your own language from a learner's point of view, some of these may come as a surprise, and seem difficult. Don't be afraid to admit your ignorance, and don't be afraid to consult your host colleagues, to whom many of these questions will be familiar. Remember, you can always go to a reference work to improve your awareness of your own language.

Chapter 3 Ten Golden Rules

Teaching English as a foreign language is a highly developed skill. A great
deal of research has been done, and although much remains to be done, some
good and bad practices have been defined. While nobody will expect you to
be an expert, confidence in the classroom will be your biggest asset, and
having a framework within which you feel comfortable will, in its turn, be the
biggest aid to your confidence. To help with that, we offer Ten Golden Rules.
Teaching is a complicated process so it is never possible to give absolute rules
which will ensure success. It is, however, possible to make some useful
generalisations which should only be breached very occasionally, and always
with a good reason. If, at any time you are teaching, you find things are not
going as you would wish, ask yourself if you are breaking any of these rules. It
will, in most cases, be wiser to maintain these general guidelines, however
difficult it may seem at a particular moment.

1 Use English all the time
The main advantage a native-speaker has in class is that it is natural for the
students to speak English to the teacher, unless the teacher reveals the fact
that she or he can also speak the student's own language. However difficult it
seems at a particular moment, it is short-sighted and counter-productive to
give away this fundamental advantage. The enforced 'naturalness' of the
students speaking English gives the teacher control in many situations where
it would otherwise be difficult. If one of the Golden Rules is to be given pre-
eminence above all the others, it is probably this one.

2 Keep it simple
At all times you should aim for simplicity – a simple approach, a simple plan,
simple language in explaining what you want, in short, simplicity in
everything. The more complicated something is, the less likely it is to succeed.
Avoid complicated lesson-plans, an over-ambitious objective, long
complicated explanations. It is always easier to expand a simple idea, rather
than trying to simplify something later.

3 Personalise, don't generalise
Part of keeping things simple is to keep them concrete, local, particular, and
most important of all, personal. Don't talk about 'what British people think',
say what *you* think. Don't ask about 'Germans', or 'Japan', ask the individual
class or individual student for an opinion. Generalisations are dangerous –
they are abstract, and frequently untrue. Part of the process of keeping things
simple is to keep them personal.

4 Be responsive
Well-organised teachers have a plan and stick to it, but a truly effective
teacher starts with a plan, but is never afraid to respond to the needs, interests

or ideas of the students. Listen to what the students have to say – in response to a particular question, of course – but also if they introduce something quite outside your general plan. It is of paramount importance that all the time you are with students you listen, listen, and listen again.

5 Be flexible
If you haven't struck oil in five minutes, stop boring! With the best will in the world you will sometimes plan a lesson for a class which is, quite simply, going to fail. Most frequently, the reason is probably that the material will be too difficult for the students. Whatever the reason, if you can feel that the class is dead, it is most unlikely to suddenly come alive. It is better to accept that things have gone wrong, and to say as simply as possible, 'I think we had better do something different', and then, make a clean break.

6 Always have a reserve plan
If you are to take the advice of the previous point, this is essential. In Chapter 11 you will find a collection of 'fillers'. Before you go into any class, make sure that you have read, and understood some or all of these, Ideally, you should try out some of them, either alone or with friends. Once you have these at your disposal, you will always have a reserve plan, and the confidence this ensures. Half a dozen fillers, which you are sure you will be able to use, will make you much more confident if anything should go wrong, and will allow you to drop your original plan, and still be sure that you have something useful and effective to do.

7 Treat each lesson separately
The most effective teaching is an extensive, coherent course. For the assistant however, it is essential to see each lesson as a separate entity because you cannot be sure you will have the same students from week to week and neither can you be sure the students will do any preparation or homework which you may set. In these circumstances, it is best to plan each lesson on the assumption that different people may be there, and students have done no pre-class preparation. But remember, each lesson should have a specific objective. Vague, general plans rarely produce effective or enjoyable lessons.

8 Don't waffle about grammar
Many native-speakers have never thought about the grammar of English from the learner's point of view, and what they have to say on the subject can sometimes be less than helpful! Many non-native teachers have an excellent knowledge of English grammar – sometimes a knowledge which exceeds their ability to speak English. In those circumstances, it is in everybody's best interest that the non-native teacher deals with the grammar in class. The native teacher can usefully advise on what is, and is not, possible English. As soon as the inexperienced native-speaker moves on to saying *why*, unhelpful waffle is likely to emerge. Most native-speaker assistants, and non-native-speaker teachers need to recognise the limitations of what the inexperienced native-speaker can say about this very complex topic.

9 Stick to what you know

As an extension of avoiding grammar waffle, it is equally helpful to avoid waffle on all other topics. Many assistants are asked questions on a wide range of topics – how language is used, aspects of British life, what is normal in contemporary Britain. Very few people are qualified to speak on such a wide range of topics with authority, common sense and due modesty! Don't try to answer what you don't know. Sometimes it is sufficient to acknowledge the value or interest of a question; stick to your experience (see rule 3 above); sometimes a simple admission of ignorance is appropriate: 'I don't know, I've never thought about that. I'm afraid I've no idea'.

10 Don't, in general, correct student's mistakes

This last Golden Rule may come as a surprise to many readers: you may think that, as a native-speaker, you can 'help' your students by correcting them when they are wrong. But this is not necessarily the case. You may be the first native-speaker that the student has spoken to – anxious, wondering if they can make themselves understood, perhaps even expecting failure. What would be most helpful to such students is the encouragement produced by success and a feeling that they can communicate, that you do understand. Research has shown that many non-native teachers over-correct their students massively, while claiming to help. In fact, they inhibit the students willingness to use broken English, and do both themselves and their students a great disservice. As a native assistant, it would be a great shame if you fell into the same pattern. For some, perhaps many, of the students you meet, you will be their first authentic occasion to use English. Just as we have advised you (see 1 above) not to throw away the naturalness of the opportunity presented by using the student's own language, so we encourage you now to be natural with the student. If you understand, respond to the message which you understand, rather than reacting to the (perhaps imperfect) language in which it is expressed. Many school students are all too aware that their teachers constantly correct them, or even perhaps jump on their mistakes. If you do not understand, don't correct or simply ask for a repeat, respond naturally by indicating what you did not understand.

Chapter 4   Will they like me?

You are not in a personality contest! Your popularity will come from
competence and from knowing what to do – or at least looking as if you do!
It's difficult to give rules for what you should and shouldn't do in a general
teaching situation. As soon as you are dealing with a group of people,
unpredictable things can happen. The following checklist will give you a
framework to help you to prepare yourself for the classes and, if things do go
wrong, it will help you to identify the cause of the problem.

Don't over-react
It's all too easy to say or do something as a reaction to what's happening
around you and later to regret it. It's very difficult to withdraw what you've
said and even more difficult to retreat from a position once you've decided to
take a stand. Think first and ask yourself not only what you're going to do
now, but how you'll handle the reaction to what you do or say. Standing in
complete silence for a few seconds is in itself usually enough to make most
students or classes cool down. Basically, your objective is very simple: to
avoid confrontation. Few students are actually 'difficult' but the urge to show
off is sometimes strong and most discipline problems are very little more than
reminding students (decisively) that what they did was rather silly or
immature, and that certainly does not involve confrontation. It's a good
guideline that the calmer and quieter you are the more likely you are to handle
the class effectively and avoid unpleasantness.

Don't aim for popularity first
The position of the assistant is rather ambiguous – not quite a teacher,
certainly not a student. In many cases, the students you are teaching will not
be very different in age from yourself and the temptation is very much to aim
for success through popularity. Your students may not expect you to be a
teacher but they will almost certainly expect you to be some sort of leader. If
you appear a competent leader and you know what you want and why you
want it and are able to ask for it in a clear and pleasant manner, you will
become popular because of your competence. Desultory chit-chat once a
week will make you unpopular, so keep lessons lively and students active.

Be explicit
In general, students respond positively to positive direction. If you are
indecisive and woolly the students will fail to respond, simply because they are
not sure what you want. This is particularly important if you change what you
want. If people start arriving for your classes later and later and you think it's
time to do something about it, don't jump on people one week if you've
tolerated the lateness the week before. Say quite clearly that you're not happy
about it and that you want people there on time the next week.

Don't forget their age

In some cases your students will have a very limited experience indeed. If they live in large towns or if they have travelled, especially abroad, they may have more to say, but don't expect those who live in small towns or in the middle of the country to have opinions and ideas about questions which are probably unfamiliar to them, even if they're eighteen years old. Try to remember what you were like at their age, and how much wider your experience and horizons are now.

Be prepared

People starting teaching for the first time tend to make two common mistakes. Firstly, they rely on spontaneity and, with the excuse of 'responding to the students' needs' go in unprepared. The most extreme version of this is one which most assistants will recognise: 'Well, what would you like to talk about this morning?' We have tried it ourselves on a number of occasions – nobody has ever wanted to talk about anything! Secondly, they over-prepare by writing out a list of topics and even a list of particular questions which can be used as a basis for the lesson. Prepare topics and even the questions by all means, but when the prepared notes become the lesson, they become so important that a spontaneous response by the teacher is lost completely and the classes become drab and dull. Contrast your own experience of lecturers who read and those who speak without reading.

Preparation covers a number of things. Make sure there is a room available for you and that it is large enough and has sufficient furniture. Find out if there is a board and chalk or pens or any other machinery you may need – perhaps a tape-recorder or overhead projector. If you're going to use a piece of machinery, make sure it works. Put tapes on the machine and find your place before the class comes into the room if at all possible. You will look and feel rather silly if you have to spin the tape backwards and forwards a dozen times while everyone sits there waiting. Remember, too, to prepare yourself. In particular make sure that the way you are dressed is suitable. Try to conform to the general standards of the staff of the school.

Admit your ignorance

Often the host teachers will know a lot more about English from a grammatical point of view than you do. Don't be afraid to admit your ignorance, either to the students or to the teachers. You can be sure that if you pretend to know something you'll be found out sooner or later.

Vary your lessons

Lessons should not always have the same format and, within the lesson, there should be a change of activity and, preferably, a change of pace from time to time. Generally, sixty minutes of the same thing is not as successful as the same sixty minutes would have been if there had been a couple of short activities before, during or after the main activity.

Keep your sense of humour

A teacher, or anyone in front of a group of people, inevitably does silly or unexpected things from time to time. They're not less funny than they would be if you were sitting in the audience. Remember if you don't laugh *with* the students they'll probably laugh *at* you.

Let your personality show

No one can respond to someone who behaves like a machine. Try to smile, say what you think yourself, take an interest in what people tell you. Don't forget that the most important thing of all is to come over as a person.

Chapter 5   Language in the classroom

Subject, medium and message

Most often, what teachers are teaching, and how they are teaching it, cannot be confused. The instructions a chemistry teacher gives are in English, but what they are talking about is chemistry. Unfortunately, when you are teaching your own language it's very easy for you and the students to confuse the different reasons that language is used in the classroom. These different reasons are:

It's the subject you're teaching
You give examples, correct, give the correct version of something students have said when they make a mistake, and so on.

It's the teaching medium
So, for example, you give instructions in English. In a situation as simple as the following you are using English in both ways:
- s: He buyed it when he was in England.
- t: Buyed?
- s: Bought.
- t: Can you say the sentence again?
- s: He bought it when he were in England.
- t: Were? *Was* – when he *was* in England.

It's the message
It is how you control students and express your relationship with them. If, for example, you say 'Did you have a nice weekend, Rita?' you can very easily be doing two different things. You are either being nice to Rita and taking a personal interest in her, or you're practising the past tense! You can only exploit the language in the classroom in this way if you are aware of what you're saying and why you're saying it.

It's you
Perhaps the biggest problem is that language is also a principal way of avoiding silence. Some teachers hate being in front of a group, with a very loud silence everywhere, so they break it by talking themselves. Unfortunately this raises two problems. Firstly, very few students will speak while you are talking, so you are actually encouraging their silence. Secondly, they are probably trying to understand what you say – they are treating what you say as either the subject or the medium. Talking to avoid silence makes the situation worse, and means that very often you have to be brave and simply keep quiet.

The worst case, which can be very funny to an observer, but not to the students, is the teacher who commentates:

> *Good morning everybody. This morning we're going to learn about how to ask people to do things for you. Now, let me see, oh dear, the board's in a mess. Where's the cloth? Just a minute now, I'll just look for the cloth. Um, can anybody see the cloth anywhere? Ah, there it is, just a moment, I'll clean up the board and then I'll put the heading up for you. There we are, now that's the board cleaned. Now, um... where's the pen? Here we are. Now... 'asking people to do things for you.'*

The teacher has said all that and, for most of the students, it has meant absolutely nothing – except that the teacher appeared confused and, worse, the class is now thoroughly confused too! What is going on? Equally tempting is to explain (to yourself) what is going to happen next:

> *Now, I'm going to give you this text and I want you to read it. And when you've read it, I'm going to ask you some questions, and I want you to answer them. So, I'll give you the text now.*

What a surprise! You may have reassured yourself, but you also confused (and probably amused) the students too.

Controlling your language

We have seen already that when you use English in the English as a foreign language classroom you are using it for several different purposes at the same time, and it's important to try to separate these. In this section we show you how to control your own language. Sometimes we present a transcription of how a teacher uses language. We have tried to present these to show stress, pauses, and so on. You will understand the effects best if you can imagine a classroom situation and read the transcripts aloud.

Giving instructions

Keep it simple. The simplest method of giving instructions is to use the imperative (but avoid shouting instructions like orders), and to use the minimum possible number of words. For example:

> *Look at me please.*
> *Don't look at your books yet, just listen.*
> *Work in pairs – you two (pointing), you two...*
> *This time listen carefully for/to...*
> *You have two or three minutes to look at that, then I'll go through it with you.*

Highlighting language

To point out a problem, an example, or an important point, pause before and then change pitch on the word or phrase. This makes it easy to separate from the flow of speech and therefore easy to follow.

> *Look at the top of page 48, there are two examples there. Listen to them: He* **knows** *her,* **doesn't** *he? He* **knows** *her,* **doesn't** *he? Here's the second one: He* **doesn't** *know her,* **does** *he? He* **doesn't** *know her,* **does** *he? Notice the verbs:* **doesn't… does… does… doesn't…** *If the main sentence is positive, the tag is negative. If the main sentence is negative, the tag is positive. Listen again. He* **doesn't** *know her,* **does** *he?* **doesn't, does**.

This is explicit. It is broken into short phrases and the important words are clearly stressed and highlighted.

Correcting

Very often when students make a mistake in spoken English they know what they should have said – it is a slip of the tongue and a long explanation is not necessary. More importantly, as we have already discussed in our Golden Rules, if you constantly correct, you will discourage the students, and throw away one of the main advantages of being a native-speaker who can respond to the message rather than the language. However, many teachers and students will expect you to correct, and simply ignoring mistakes can make you seem careless, or even irresponsible.

Modern language teaching theory and research suggests that much correcting does not in fact help students, and may even be counter-productive. A much better technique is available so that you respond to the mistake, but without obviously correcting it. The technique is called *reformulation* and is what most of us do naturally in conversation. It is worth explaining the distinction carefully. In traditional language teaching, correcting was based on the fact that the student made a mistake, and the teacher's primary objective was to get the student who made the mistake to say the correct sentence. As a result, a dialogue like this was considered good technique

T: Where did he buy it?
S: He buyed it from London.
T: (Raises eyebrows, makes a gesture)
S: In London?
T: Yes, good, but not *buyed…*
S: Bought.
T: Yes that's right. So, where did he buy it?
S: He bought it in London.
T: Good.

The underlying assumption was that the student learned to make correct sentences by saying correct sentences, so it was important that the correct sentence was repeated by the student. The theory was that unless this was done, the mistake may become ingrained. However, modern research and theory now suggests that the student will be helped most in the long run if the teacher reacts to the message in a comparatively natural way. If you understand what the student says, but it contains wrong language, repeat a natural version of the same content, but not the exact language.

T: Where did he buy it?
S: He buyed it from London.
T: Oh, he bought it in London did he? Where exactly?

Notice the teacher reformulates what the student said, introducing the correct language items, but without unnaturalness, and, most importantly, without requiring the student to repeat a correct answer just for the sake of it. Using reformulation, rather than formal correction is more helpful to your classes, and produces a more natural, and relaxed atmosphere which is more likely to encourage your students to want to talk to you.

Explaining vocabulary

Explaining vocabulary need not necessarily be done linguistically. For example, you don't need to give a dictionary definition of 'a watch' while wearing one! Besides, you are not usually explaining to the students what, for example, a watch is. Frequently you are only telling them the word, not explaining anything. Translation is one way of explaining, but we have discussed why it's not a good idea for you to reveal to the class how much of their language you know, although in a few cases translation is inevitable. Here are some useful ways of explaining vocabulary:

Demonstration
grin, angry, hop, stagger
Most verbs, most nouns, and many adjectives can be explained in this way.

Drawing
slim, tree, bush, yacht
A quick sketch with a few lines is sufficient – it only has to show the essential details.

Opposites
If you are single you're not married.
Jack is polite, but his brother is rude.
They do not need to be logical opposites in the strict sense. In the same way as the *tree/bush* drawings, the secret is to contrast two words, one the class knows and the new word to highlight the difference.

Synonyms
Huge means very big.
Plump means fat.
You don't always have to give an exact synonym. The idea is to give the students the general meaning of the word.

19

Definitions
An optician is a person who tests your eyes and tells you if you need glasses.
It's usually much more difficult to give definitions than to use definitions or synonyms.

Give a context
Someone who doesn't say 'sorry' when he or she bumps into you is rude.
Someone is rude when they don't apologise when they're late or if they push past you in a crowd.
Always give several contexts to make sure the word is not misunderstood.

Translation
oak, measles, alsatian
This is mostly used for words which are 'a kind of dog/disease/etc.' Even here if you want to avoid speaking the students' language in class you can say to one of them, 'Could you look that up in the dictionary for us, please. What's the (German) word for it?'

Explaining grammar

To explain a grammar point or what we say in a given situation can be more difficult than explaining vocabulary. However, there are tactics to reduce the amount of language you use. The most important are:

Questions and answers
Ask yourself a question and answer it: 'Why do we use *any* in this sentence, not *some*? It's because the sentence is negative.' With advanced classes you can use the question and answer technique by asking the class the same sort of questions. If someone in the class answers, it saves you explaining something they already know and gives them a chance to talk, instead of you. But if you ask the class the general question 'What does … mean?' you will almost never get an answer, even if they do know. It is very difficult to define words in a foreign language. Your questions should always be of the kind, 'Why do we say/use *excuse me* here, not *sorry*?' Thus the answer students have to give is linguistically simple, even if the idea behind it is quite difficult.

Draw attention to an example in context
'Did you notice what I/he said?' or 'Did you notice what it said in the text?' This needs very little language indeed: 'When we want to ask if we can do something, we say *Do you mind if I …*'

Present the relevant part
When you are presenting grammar, present only the part that is relevant to the problem. Make simple statements that are true but perhaps not the whole truth. Try to say something the students can use without worrying if it is complete. Say as little as possible, as concisely as possible. If the language of the explanation is more difficult than the point you are explaining, something is wrong.

Doing exercises

In this effective presentation of the exercise below, notice how little the teacher says.

Look at these two patterns:

    Do you mind if I have a chocolate?

    Would you mind if I had a chocolate?

Use those two patterns when you want to:

1 Phone someone later.

2 Use the telephone.

3 Leave early.

4 Put the light on.

5 Take it home with you.

6 Ring a friend.

7 Smoke.

8 Have some more.

T: So, notice if it starts with 'do' it's followed by the present,,, '*Do* you mind if I *have*...', but if it starts with 'would' it's followed by the past... '*Would* you mind if I *had*.' Now look at the exercise. Can you do the first one please, Maurice? Start with 'do'.

S1: Do you mind if I phone you later?

T: Good. The same one, Danielle. Start with 'would', please.

S2: Would you mind if I phone you later?

T: It's the past if you start with 'would'. Do it again please.

S3: Would you mind if I phoned you later?

T: Good. Number 2, Robert. Start 'do'...

If you listen to one of the good television news-readers, not only do they sound relatively spontaneous but it is also easy to hear when they change from one item to another or when, for example, they quote somebody else's words. Because you're using language for several different reasons, often at the same time, you must change your voice too. Make plenty of pauses and change the pitch. Think, for example, how you would say: 'No, not buyed, bought, I bought it in Paris.'

Said on a monotone, it's impossible to understand either what you mean or what you want the student to do. Use your voice, and in particular use pauses, to make it clear.

With exercises which require a personal response, each example can be used several times. Exercises like this have more opportunity for some humour and, if the opportunity for a little conversation arises, interrupt the exercise for a couple of minutes chat and then return to it, as in the following example.

> Start your answer with 'I'll probably …'
> What will you do:
> 1 If it rains tomorrow.
> 2 When you get home this evening.
> 3 At the weekend.
> 4 If you feel ill in the morning.
> 5 Next summer.
> 6 If you win a lot of money.

T: So if we want to talk about something we're not sure about, something that might happen, we can use 'I'll probably…' . Let's look at the exercise. Can you do number one, please, Maria?

S1: (silence).

T: If it rains tomorrow what will you do? Start 'I'll probably…'

S1: I'll probably, er, I'll probably bring my umbrella.

T: Good. Can you say something different, Mario?

S2: I'll probably stay at home.

T: Oh you will, will you? Have a day off school, um hum. Can you do number two then please? Yes, you again, Mario.

S2: I'll probably go to sleep, I'm tired.

T: Very good, Mario. The same one, Antonio.

S3: I'll probably have something to eat.

T: Good – The same one then, Laura.

S4: I'll probably go to see my grandmother.

T: Good. Number 3, Silvio…

When you respond to a student's answer, your response should be appropriate in two ways – both as a teacher (by, for example, correcting them or following up with a further question) and as a person. Try to avoid making this sort of mistake:

T: Do you go to the cinema very often?

S1: No, not really.

T: What about you, Maria?

S2: Yes, quite often.

T: How often?

S2: Oh, about once a week.

T: What about you, Giorgio?

S3: No, not much. But I was in a film once.

T: Oh, were you? And what about you, Marco?

S4: I prefer to watch television.

The student who volunteered 'I was in a film once.' is not going to say much more if all the teacher says is 'Oh, were you?' Take a normal human interest in what students say!

We are not suggesting that you control your language as some kind of theoretical principle, but it's of direct practical help to you in the classroom. The occasional word, gesture and particularly eye movement, are often much better than a lot of talk from the teacher. If you find yourself talking too much, look back at the tactics suggested above. Perhaps the most important principle of all is not to be afraid to be quiet. If you are silent the students may find something interesting to say.

Some language you could teach

If you ask your host colleagues what they expect you to do, they will probably answer 'conversation' and 'spoken English', seeing these as synonymous. However, there is a whole area that we can define as 'spoken English', which they will find difficulty in teaching, but which you are ideally suited to teach. It is the area of everyday English – what to say to build normal relationships in normal situations. In speech we show our attitudes to each other in our use of a whole set of words, phrases, and structures, *I'm sorry, I'm afraid, anyway.* The misuse of such phrases can often be a cause of misunderstanding. The average learner is often better at producing grammatically correct sentences than at producing appropriate ones.

It is not uncommon for people to come over as quite different when speaking a foreign language and in teaching this sort of functional language, it is more important than ever to remember that speaking a foreign language is very different from speaking your own. As native-speakers we instinctively know what language is appropriate, and we can predict the effect it will have on others. Our choice of language, like dress, is also a means of expressing our personality. A teacher of language must do two things: explain the effect of a piece of language – what assumptions the listener will make about the speaker's age, attitudes, and personality, and teach the kind of language which matches the age and attitudes of the learner. In class you should teach the kind of language which will be most generally acceptable, and since most foreign learners use their language to relative strangers such as taxi-drivers and shop assistants, your aim should be to present them with a slightly more formal register than you would use yourself.

Classes will find this work all the more enjoyable if you use as much of the language given in this section as often and as naturally as you can around the classroom. Never, for example, open a window yourself. Ask the class what you should say to get one of the students to open it for you. Encourage students to look for situations to use the language they have learned.

If you merely present the language in this section by writing it on the board and explaining it, you have not *taught* it. Here is a possible sequence of activities:

1   Describe a situation: 'Someone has just stopped you in the street and said to you, *Excuse me, could you tell me the time please?* You haven't got a watch. What do you say?'

2 Comment on the responses, saying why they are appropriate or inappropriate. For example, 'No, that's much too intimate/formal etc.'.
3 Agree on a suitable response. Get the class to repeat the phrase several times, both in and out of context.
4 Build up a simple dialogue.

Putting the language in context

Situations

Here is a list of everyday situations where a learner can practise and learn the language used. You can write simple dialogues for all these situations.

- Buying a ticket at the railway station.
- Buying a hamburger.
- Buying stamps.
- Changing money.
- Buying a cinema ticket.
- Shopping – buying a film, shirt, pair of shoes, can of drink etc.
- At the chemist's – explaining what's wrong.
- At the police station – explaining that you have lost your camera (for example), describing it and where you think you lost it.

Functions

The following is a list of some of the most important functions a foreigner might need when speaking English. When writing dialogues around these functions, don't make your language too informal or too formal. An example of the first one is given.

1 Starting a conversation.
A: Oh hello, how are you?
B: Fine thanks, and you?
A: Very well, thank you.
B: Terrible day, isn't it?
A: Yes, horrible, isn't it.

2 Inviting people
Would you like to...? I'd love to. That'd be nice.

3 Making suggestions
Let's... Why don't we...? What about ...ing? That's a good idea.

4 Making a plan together
Shall we...? Why don't we...? What a good idea.

5 Asking for help
Excuse me, could you...? Would you...? Please. Certainly.

6 Asking for, giving and refusing permission
Do you mind if I...? Not at all. May I...? Certainly. I'd rather you didn't...

7 Asking for and giving advice
What do you think I should do? Do you think it's a good idea? If I were you I'd...
Have you thought of...? Why don't you...?

8 Agreeing and disagreeing (informal)
What did you think of...? That's exactly what I thought.
Well, actually, I thought it was...

9 Agreeing and disagreeing (more formal)
I agree with you completely. I really can't agree with that.

10 Asking for and offering things
Could I have a... please? I'd like a... Would you like a...? Yes please.
No, thank you.

11 Asking for and giving directions
Excuse me, I wonder if you could tell me the way to... please. Go straight along ...
down up ... turn right ... turn left ... take the second on the right ... it's on the left
... opposite the ... You can't miss it. I'm sorry, I'm a stranger here myself.

Important words and phrases

Here is a list of some of the most important phrases of spoken English. We give examples of each with explicit classroom explanations.

Thank you/thanks
Used only for something unimportant. If someone does something particularly generous or something you wouldn't expect, you need to use something stronger such as *Thank you very much, that was kind of you.* or *Thank you, I am grateful.*

Sorry
Used after you have inconvenienced somebody slightly.
The normal answer to *Sorry* is *Sorry.*
For something more serious we use: *I am sorry.* or *I'm so sorry.* often followed by an explanation *(I'm afraid I didn't notice it, I'm afraid I wasn't listening).*
To answer a real apology like this, we use: *Don't worry, that's quite all right.*

Sorry? Pardon?
Used if you would like the other person to repeat what they have said for any reason (you didn't hear/understand/believe).
I beg your pardon is now rather old-fashioned.
What? or *What did you say?* are very informal and are mostly reserved for informal situations.

Excuse me
Used if you wish to pass somebody.

Excuse me...?
Used before you ask assistance or information from somebody.
Remember the basic rule in English: *Excuse me* before you do something,
Sorry after you do something.

Please...
This can be used in three places in spoken English:
- At the end of requests: *Could you pass me that book please?*
- At the beginning of invitations: *Please don't wait for me. Please sit down.*
- In the middle in situations where the speaker demands (often used when asking for the second time): *Could you please remember to bring it tomorrow?*

Really?
Sorry? is used to ask the other person to repeat the same thing. In a similar way *Really?* is used to mean *Can you give me more details?* and also for showing an interest in what the other person is saying.

Would you?/Have you?/Are you? etc.
These are used in order to show interest and invite further details. The auxiliary verb used is appropriate to the one used by the previous speaker:
- A: We went up to London at the weekend.
- B: Did you?

Yes. No.
These are only used alone if it is absolutely clear to both speakers that only the information in what is being said is important. Normally such one-word answers are avoided. Suitable alternatives are:
Yes, please. Yes, thank you. Yes, that's right. Yes, we did/have etc.
No, I'm afraid not. I'm afraid we haven't/didn't/etc. No, not yet. No, not quite.

I'm afraid...
This is used in all situations when giving other people information which they may/could interpret as negative or unhelpful. In other words, it is used to make negative responses sound less abrupt:
I'm afraid I haven't. I'm afraid we don't. I'm afraid we will.

It is easy to give an impression of unhelpfulness if you omit this when making negative responses.

Really...
When using weak or uninteresting positive adjectives we normally add *really*; the sentence without *really* will usually be interpreted negatively by the listener.
She's a nice girl (but ...)
She's a really nice girl.

Not very + a positive adjective

It is rather rare in informal conversational English to use negative adjectives except in very informal situations. Sentences like *He's short.* or *She's ugly.* sound rude. We often prefer *not very* with the corresponding positive adjective.
It's not a very interesting job.
It wasn't very well typed.

Conversational tactics

Question tags

This area is more misunderstood by teachers and learners of English than almost any other. It is also an area where you can put your native fluency to good use. The two most common kinds of tags are:

1 *It's next Saturday, isn't it?*
Said with rising intonation, this is a question and needs an answer.
   A: You've been to Italy, haven't you?
   B: Oh yes, we were in Rome last year at Easter.

2 *It's next Saturday, isn't it.*
Said with a falling intonation, this is not a question; it is an invitation to the other speaker to comment and develop the conversation about the topic proposed.
   A: You can't speak French, can you.
   B: Well as a matter of fact I can. I spent a year in France when I was a student.

Non-native teachers very often teach all tags as question tags, and seldom differentiate between those which are questions requiring an answer, and those which are conversational gambits, requiring a response. A particularly common use of the latter is at the beginning of a conversation to talk about the weather:
   A: Lovely day, isn't it.
   B: Yes, marvellous, isn't it.

These are not and cannot be questions. When the learner of English answers those tags like questions the effect can be very odd indeed:
   A: You've been here before, haven't you.
   B: Yes, I have.
   A: It's a nice place for a holiday, isn't it.
   B: Yes, it is.
   A: And you can always depend on the weather, can't you.
   B: Yes, you can.

Here *B* is only answering. A longer answer developing the conversation would be more appropriate.

The rules for making tags structurally are straightforward:

Positive sentences have negative tags.
Negative sentences have positive tags.

If the main sentence contains an auxiliary verb, the (first) auxiliary is used again in the tag: *They should be able to come, shouldn't they?*

If there is no auxiliary verb – the sentence is either present simple or past simple – the appropriate part of *do* (*do, does, did*) is used in the tag:
They went last year, didn't they?
He speaks French, doesn't he?
You know them, don't you?

Expanding a response

The form of tags is easily practised in the classroom. Exercises usually take the form:
   T: She can swim.
   CLASS: Can't she?
or better:
   T: They're married.
   CLASS: They're married, aren't they?

However, this is very unnatural. If this is all the teacher does, the students do not get the idea that a tag is only the first step in a conversation. They must also learn the second step, how to respond fully.
Look at the following possible responses:
   You've been to Italy, haven't you?
   a) *Yes.*
   b) *Yes, I have.*
   c) *Yes, I have as a matter of fact. I was there last year.*
   d) *Yes, I have as a matter of fact – in Naples.*
   e) *Yes, I have as a matter of fact. Have you?*

Notice that a) and b) treat the statement as if it were a question: they only answer it. In a conversation they would be seen by a native-speaker as 'blocking' remarks. He or she would assume that the other person did not wish to pursue the subject of Italy for some reason. However, the others are all natural friendly responses which make a positive contribution to the conversation.

Natural responses

In natural English, *Yes* and *No* used alone are relatively rare. Much more common are responses involving the repetition of the auxiliary verb of the previous speaker, for example:
   A: Do you know Viv?
   B: Yes, I do./No, I don't.
   A: Does she go out much?
   B: Yes, she does./No, she doesn't.
   A: It's ready, isn't it?
   B: Yes, it is./No, I'm afraid it isn't.

Very often these short responses are followed by *actually* or *as a matter of fact.*

It's worth pointing out to classes that the difference between a one word answer (*Yes.*) and a fuller answer (*Yes, it is actually.*) can make the difference between natural and unnatural English and the difference between people thinking you are a normal, friendly person or rather abrupt. In our experience the idea that language is something personal is important and, as students begin to understand this, it makes lessons more interesting, more relevant and more fun.

We use a very similar pattern to encourage the other person to talk:
  A: I've just been to London.
  B: Oh, have you?
  A: I took my driving test last week.
  B: Oh, did you?

Another similar pattern is used to show agreement:
  A: I'd love to visit London.
  B: So would I.
  B: But I wouldn't like to go in the winter.
  A: No, neither would I.

And finally, a similar pattern can be used to say no in a pleasant way:
  A: Can you change a pound, please?
  B: I'm sorry, I'm afraid I can't.
  A: Do you know if there's a bank near here please?
  B: I'm sorry, I'm afraid I don't.

We have discussed a number of different language points in this chapter, and some of them will not be of particular use to you in your teaching, depending on the situation in which you find yourself. The main point is that you should plan your conversation lessons, and not go into the classroom with the idea that conversation will just happen naturally. If you have a clear idea of the information contained in this chapter for yourself, you may be able to introduce it into appropriate points in you lessons. Often it will be appropriate when you want to correct or help a student, and it may be of particular importance if you are working in a team-teaching situation with a non-native teacher.

Chapter 6   Your basic lesson

Planning a lesson

In our Golden Rules section, we stressed the importance of treating each lesson as a separate entity, and that advice holds good. It is not true, however, that every lesson needs to be devised from scratch. A few basic lesson formats will cover the majority of lessons. On page 33 we propose a lesson-plan which should provide the basis for any lesson you do.

Reports from returning assistants reveal that many of them tend to use a single idea for a lesson based on a song, a text, a piece of video etc. They then dive straight in, trying despairingly to get the students involved in the theme, or to talk about the song, text etc. This approach is likely to cause difficulties.

In the Golden Rules, we suggested that you should always have a reserve plan and one or more fillers, (see Chapter 11). You can use fillers either if things go wrong, or if the material runs out earlier than you expected. If you have a successful lesson, you may still want to use them for variety or change of pace. Most fillers do not require material, but it is important that you understand how they work, and that you have mentally prepared in case you need them. Some are more suitable for one level or size of group than another, and it is therefore helpful before going into class, to have made a note on your lesson-plan of the fillers that you think might be appropriate to this lesson. You may not use them, but the safety net will reassure you, and give you the confidence to treat the main item in a more relaxed, and therefore probably more successful way. The remainder of the lesson merely expands the single key item – song, text, tape etc. – into three parts. In practice, the three parts may not be as distinct as the plan suggests, but it does provide you with a coherent way of preparing the subject matter before you go into class.

Stages of a lesson

Introduction
Students may be arriving in an English class from chemistry, or games. It may be early in the morning, just before lunch, or late in the day. The students may not be fully alert, and there is certainly no reason why they should be 'tuned in' to English.

Introduce the topic by talking a little yourself first. Remember the Golden Rule – *personalise, don't generalise*, so talk about the topic from your own point of view, experience or interest. If you can't talk about it, it's unreasonable to expect the students to do so!

The introduction may be only brief – perhaps a couple of minutes, certainly not longer than five, but try not to miss it out. It sets the scene in terms of content, raises the students' interest, and, ideally, introduces some of the key vocabulary and ideas which will come up in the text, tape or whatever.

Generally, the introduction should consist of you talking, and the students listening, and perhaps responding either as a group, or as individuals. The main point is that you dictate what happens and the speed at which it happens. It is important to get the lesson off to a good start, and to avoid starting with a limp and deadening remark like 'Today we are going to talk about…' or 'Now, can you look at this text.' Done well, the introduction can make the rest of the lesson much easier and more productive. Your enthusiasm for a topic or activity can, and should, enthuse the class.

Presentation

Too often, assistants try to get the students to talk when the students do not have the language or the ideas that are needed to respond positively. You will find it much easier to get a response and much greater job satisfaction, if you try to ensure that in each lesson something is *presented*. You can use a song, text, a short piece of video, a story, an article, an advert, almost any piece of linguistic material may be appropriate. Usually, the piece should be short – shorter probably than you expect – certainly not more than one page of text, but perhaps only a paragraph; in the case of a piece of tape maybe only a six or ten line dialogue; in the case of a piece of video, perhaps only five minutes of actual video. The fundamental skill you need to develop is the ability to use this small piece of input as the basis for your lesson. Usually the presentation will introduce some language – either new or for revision – and some content or ideas – something worth talking about. This is the basis of the lesson, but absolutely not the lesson itself. The idea is to activate the student's interest and language in response to this material; stimulating a response to something presented should be easier than simply expecting the students to talk.

Exploitation

This part of the lesson is what you would probably try to do naturally – getting the students to talk, use the new language, discuss the ideas in a text or video etc. This is the important part of the lesson, but it should always be preceded by an introduction and presentation, and you should always try to have the safety net of a filler to follow it. If you follow this basic approach you are much more likely to be successful than if you dive in cold.

There are many different ways in which material can be both presented and exploited, but what you need are a few basic techniques for turning an idea, or a concrete piece of material into a lesson. The next chapter suggests some basic ways of doing this.

The first lesson

If you have never met the class before, it is best to have a standard first lesson, with simple and limited objectives. The most important aim in a first lesson is for you to come over as a real person. This means deciding what you are going to do before you go in, then going in, preferably with no material, and looking at the students. As soon as you take your eyes off them you lose contact, and if you do not come across as a person they may lose interest. Your main aim should be to make them want to come back to your next session. Ideally, we suggest you work without material, keeping the following points in mind:

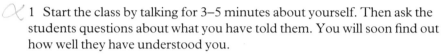

1 Start the class by talking for 3–5 minutes about yourself. Then ask the students questions about what you have told them. You will soon find out how well they have understood you.

2 Make the class active. Many classes will not be used to speaking English and if you can make them speak to each other in your first lesson, they will be all the more positive to you. Put some questions on the board and get the students to interview each other in pairs. For example:
Which part of the town do you live in?
What are you interested in outside school?
What do you like to do at the weekends?
Have you ever been to England?
Have you ever spoken to any other English person?

While students are working in pairs, walk around the class all the time listening and making sure that they are speaking English. Make it clear when you want them to stop (clap once loudly!) then get some of them to report what they have found out about their friend.

3 Establish at the start that English will be the only language you allow in the room. Then teach the class something obviously useful that they do not already know. For example, teach at any level what to say to you the next time they see you – students tend to find this ritual greeting difficult:
Hello, how are you?
Fine thanks, and you?
Very well, thank you.

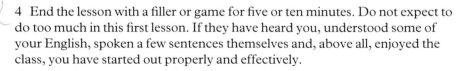

4 End the lesson with a filler or game for five or ten minutes. Do not expect to do too much in this first lesson. If they have heard you, understood some of your English, spoken a few sentences themselves and, above all, enjoyed the class, you have started out properly and effectively.

A lesson-plan template

		Time
Introduction from teacher		minimum 2-3 mins; maximum 5
Presentation	Individual or group work	
Exploitation		
Fillers	Prepare two or three suitable ones – short and long, but use only one, depending on available time.	

Chapter 7   Developing lessons

Contingency plan.

Once you have a basic idea, or a piece of material – text, tape or video – the most difficult thing is to turn that into a lesson. As we have already said, you need a filler and a short, probably personal introduction. The substance of the lesson, however, is the presentation/exploitation stage. In this chapter we list a number of basic ways in which an idea or piece of material can be developed for the central part of the lesson. If you only try to have a conversation with a class, you will find yourself in more difficulty than if you have some techniques, such as the ones in this chapter, which will help you to teach a little more English. These techniques will make you both more confident and more competent, and make your classes more effective and more enjoyable.

Teaching a whole class

Assistants find themselves in many different situations, although in theory they should only be teaching small groups drawn from the basic class. It can be rather intimidating if you are faced with a whole class of thirty students. There is a temptation to talk at the class, and hope for some response. Even with a good class, however, it is difficult for an individual to respond, and there is an obvious danger that the two or three best students in the class will dominate everything. While this may 'save' your lesson, it is not going to help the majority of students and is very un-relaxing for you.

Break the class down

If you are faced with a whole class you can always divide it into smaller groups. It is much better for part of the lesson to be conducted with students working individually, in pairs or small groups, speaking to each other rather than to you. Even in a fairly small class, well-prepared material for the presentation part of the lesson is frequently done most effectively by allowing the students to work in this way.

Quiet preparation can be well-invested time. Your lessons are more likely to be effective if they are not all just you in front of the whole class. You may be anxious that breaking the class down in this way may mean that you could lose control, but this will certainly not happen providing the students are given a task to perform, they have clearly understood what they have to do before working in pairs or groups, and providing the task is not too difficult for them. Pair or group work is an ideal way for students to prepare before the second phase of the lesson in which they report back in a whole class activity. This preparation and reporting back mirrors the presentation/exploitation division which we have already suggested.

Individual preparation

Give students a chance to prepare, both ideas and language. But remember, this preparation must be based on something concrete – the piece of paper which is given to the students at the beginning of the lesson.

Appropriate activities for individual work include:
- Reading through a text
- Completing a questionnaire
- Completing a text, drawing, etc.
- Collecting known words
- Looking up new words in a dictionary
- Preparing questions, to ask either the teacher or other students

Almost anything which can be prepared individually can also be done in pairs. This has the advantage that a better student can help a weaker one, and that there will, inevitably, be some talking in or about English. Don't worry if much of what you hear is students using their own language – it is important to remember that this part of the lesson is preparation, and you are hoping to activate their English later.

After students have done an activity individually, before doing the activity as a whole class, it can be useful to let them talk to their neighbours in pairs – this time in English. Students who are unwilling to speak even to their neighbour, are certainly not going to be happy speaking in front of the whole class. Don't expect too much too soon.

Group work

Sometimes it is ideal to put students into rather larger groups – anything from three to six students – larger than six tends not to be effective. If you do put students into groups, it is always a good idea to appoint one student to take notes, so that they are doing, and producing something. While the group work is taking place, you should move quietly and in a friendly way from group to group, but not necessarily take an active part in what they are doing. There are several good reasons for getting students to work in groups: more students get the chance to speak in a lower stress situation, and you do not have to try to stimulate all thirty students at the same time! Moreover, the shyer students get something to do, in a mode in which they are more likely to feel comfortable.

Appropriate activities for group work include:
- Different groups read different parts of the same text that you have copied and cut up.
- Different groups answer different questions before reporting back to the whole class.
- Groups work competitively, for example, trying to do a matching exercise or complete a word partnership box (see page 39).

How much material?

If you lack experience, the temptation is to take as much material as possible into the room and hide behind the material. There are many reasons why this is not a good idea:

- Too much material will confuse you, as well as the students.
- You will tend to rush, which means students will not understand.
- The material will take over from you, and you should be the most interesting thing in the room!

Expanding nothing is better than compressing too much. Ironically, the more nervous you are, the less material we would advise you to take in. We have already stressed the importance of responding personally to the students and appearing a person yourself, and it requires a lot of experience to do this if there is so much material that you are hidden behind it. Providing you follow the advice of preparing some suitable fillers, you should have the confidence to take in a small piece of material, which you and the students can expand together. A corollary to this is that it is much better to use material which is too easy rather than too difficult. Anybody can make material more difficult simply by adding additional questions, or widening the theme. One of the most difficult things for any teacher to do is to simplify material in the classroom which is actually above the students' heads.

In preparing this book, we consulted a lot of former assistants and one of the things they emphasised was how difficult it had been to accept the advice that a little, simple material was better than a lot of complicated material. If you are sceptical of our advice, at least take that of your returning colleagues, many of whom learned the hard way that this advice is practical.

Materials and activities

Student input

Any lesson which is based on student input is more likely to be effective than anything that the teacher can devise. Everyone, even the youngest student, has something to bring to the class – their own ideas, experience, likes, dislikes, and personal information. It is important that you do not over-estimate students' experience or language ability, but it is equally important to realise that you must not underestimate them either. Sometimes students may raise a matter spontaneously, in which case you should pick up and develop the interest that they show. More frequently, you may want to try and organise the lessons so that the students can make some input. This can be done in a number of ways:

- Ask students to prepare questions – for example, to ask you about a particular topic, or to ask each other.
- Ask students in groups to prepare questions for a questionnaire, which you then photocopy and give to other students in the class in a subsequent lesson.

- Students try to tell a favourite joke in English.
- Students complete a personal questionnaire where each student is the only person who knows the answer to those questions. For example,
  What is your grandmother's name?
  What colour you would like to paint your own room?
  Who is the weirdest person you have ever met?

If you prepare a questionnaire of this kind, it is best to include one or two questions at the end which are as open as possible – here are some examples:
Write the name of a famous person you would like to meet. Write one question you would ask him/her.
Write five adjectives that say how you feel today.
Some words often go together – 'interesting book, funny story'. Write down three adjective/noun pairs which seem crazy, but which mean something to you.

Rather than just trying to teach them the correct grammar of English, with the emphasis on getting things right, look for anything which interests or amuses the students. The more imaginative and open your approach, and the more you invite, encourage and positively value student input, the more likely you are to be successful.

Jigsaw and information-gap activities

Language teaching often uses two similar ideas – the jigsaw, and the information-gap. Whenever we use language in real life there is an information-gap: we ask for information that we need, but do not have, or we offer our view or opinion to someone who we think does not already know it. The gap may be a matter of fact as in: 'Could you tell me the time of the last bus, please?' or simply a matter of opinion, as when, for example, you would like to know what your friend thought of the film which you have both just seen together. In the classroom, natural information-gaps also occur but it is also possible to create them, by giving one student certain information, for example a timetable, the entertainments page out of the newspaper, or a menu, and giving the other student a paper which lists information they must find out: a good way to spend Saturday evening, or a meal suitable for a vegetarian. Information-gap activities are particularly suitable for pair work.

Jigsaw activities are similar in that the teacher takes something which is whole – for example, a text – photocopies it, and then cuts it into pieces. The students' task, either individually or in groups, is to put the whole back together again. A text cut into pieces paragraph by paragraph, or a dialogue cut into 'turns' are suitable for this sort of activity. Jigsaw activities are particularly suitable for the presentation part of the lesson, and may lead to further whole class discussion work based on a text, prepared in pairs or small groups.

Students listen and respond

Every student has sat in lessons where the teacher talked, and talked and talked. You droning on is unlikely to be of any interest to anybody, but it is a great temptation when you have a captive audience! It is perfectly legitimate, however, indeed very useful to your students, if you can talk to them in a *controlled* way. Modern language teaching theory tells us that the best way to learn is to listen carefully. We all learned our first language by listening, not by talking.

When you are talking and students are listening, several points need to be borne in mind:
- Don't babble, ramble or mumble.
- Don't speak for very long at one time. Two or three minutes is often enough, five is almost always too long.
- Don't talk about abstract things – in particular, not about grammar.
- Remember the rule: *Personalise, don't generalise.*
- Ensure students are active – you must not talk so they can go to sleep. They must be given some questions before you begin, either on paper or on the board, which they have to answer from what you say. The idea is you talk and they respond, not you talk!
- Paraphrase yourself. Don't repeat yourself exactly, but try to say everything two or three times in slightly different words. This is not something we normally do, and it is not natural English, but it is excellent exposure for students. An example is given below.

> *I come from Canterbury. It's in the south of England, not the north. It's not in the north of England – a long way from London, it's in the south. It's not far from London. It's about 40 miles, but that's not far. It's in the south-east corner of England. It's a very old town. It has a beautiful old cathedral. In fact the cathedral is one of the most important churches in England. The cathedral is very old. It's at least 700 years old but some parts of the town are very new. The parts near the cathedral are protected – they are historic buildings, so we can't pull them down and build new buildings. There are quite a lot of beautiful old buildings near the cathedral, but the main part of the town is new and modern. Canterbury is a nice mixture of the old and the new. We get a lot of visitors, especially from France. The ferries from France come to Dover and those are not far from Canterbury. Lots of French people come over to England just for the day to look at the shops. Some of those French people come to Canterbury. We have a lot of tourists in Canterbury from all over the world. Of course most of them come to see the cathedral ...*

Notice particularly the short sentences, the recycling, the frequent oppositions (*not old ... new*); paraphrasing and use of synonyms (*new ... modern*).

For a very low-level class, perhaps in their first or second year of English, give students three or four questions on the board, or on a piece of paper, and ask them to listen for the answer while you are talking, and then after you have stopped give them a moment or two to write out their answers. At more advanced levels a similar technique can be used. Either you talk about much more complex topics, or you can even use a news bulletin, or a piece of video – the basic technique is the same, the students listen and respond.

From here

Word-partnerships

You can easily develop one technique which you can use again and again with classes at many different levels which will almost always provide you with an activity which will use a few minutes usefully, in a way which is new for students.

Try the following yourself – do you think you 'know' the word *bus*? The temptation is to say 'Of course', and indeed most of your students will say the same. But what makes you able to use this word is the fact that you know the other words which regularly co-occur with it – the regular word-partnerships that it forms. Can you, before reading on, write down five adjectives which regularly occur immediately before the word *bus*? Can you also list five verbs which you can use in front of *bus*? You will find that even quite advanced students cannot do this – they will make impossible combinations, and not know some of the most common. As a result, if you can identify any important nouns, you can do a few minutes useful work by asking them first individually, then in pairs or small groups to gather together, for example, five adjectives, and five verbs which form partnerships. Instead of just asking students to make lists of new words you can help considerably by getting them to record the words in partnerships, as in the box below.

catch	last	
miss	next	
wait for	first	bus
get	local	
take	express	

When doing this activity, make sure you have thought of some words before you go into the class. It is actually quite difficult to think of words yourself while you are standing in front of the class. Do not underestimate the difficulty of this exercise – even quite advanced students will have trouble doing it.

A similar sort of exercise, which you can prepare in advance and which can be done at any level, involves breaking five word-partnerships into parts and then asking the students to put the five parts back together in natural pairs. Here are two examples:

ride	a car
play	a calculator
drive	the piano
cook	a bike
use	a meal

integrate	concern
tackle	a minority
summarise	action
express	a problem
take	the position

Don't underestimate the difficulty of this exercise. It may be obvious to you, as a native-speaker but it is certainly not obvious to a student that, for example, you *ride* rather than *drive* a bike – we simply know these combinations as a result of meeting them very frequently.

Brain-storming

Very often students are expected to produce full sentences in correct English, but this is actually quite difficult. You can make a more relaxed beginning to a lesson, and involve more students by using the brain-storming technique. Almost anything can be brain-stormed and organised. Students call out all the words or ideas that come to mind, perhaps linked to a particular theme, without organising them in any way. The teacher simply lists all the items that are called out on the board, or an overhead transparency sheet. Once the words or ideas have been collected in this way, allowing students to contribute in different ways, with different degrees of difficulty, and without comment or criticism from the teacher, the material is used in some way by being organised – either by the teacher, or the students working in small groups. This technique is not quiet and orderly, and you may feel it is a bit risky. However, we assure you that it will involve more students, in a more lively way than any traditional conversation class and it also provides an excellent introduction to the lesson because it brings words and ideas into the room without criticism, before the more serious work begins.

You could ask the students to call out:
- All the words they know to do with transport.
- All the words for describing people.
- All the words they know beginning with *b*.
- All the verbs they know for playing sports or games.
- All the words they know that rhyme with *hat*.
- All the words they know that can fill the space in the sentence *Oh dear, I feel…*
- All the good things they can think of about television.
- All the problems you have if you have no money.
- All the things you need to take with you if you are going on holiday to the seaside.

The whole point of brain-storming is to use random volunteered responses – to let students call out what they wish, when they wish, without comment from you. You simply record what is said on the board or transparency. It is the introductory part of the lesson, and the material collected will be used later – don't exclude mistakes, silly suggestions, misunderstandings etc. at the brain-storming stage. For this quite short phase of the lesson, anything goes! If it sounds a bit intimidating, try it one day with a class which is normally rather quiet – it's fun, it works, and it is also useful.

Speaking practice

Use speaking practice to change the pace of a lesson. This suggestion is rather different from the others in this chapter, which are all techniques which can be applied to different material, and different lessons. For most students, practising pronunciation or oral grammar is probably not particularly useful: most students over the age of eleven are not good mimics any more, and pronunciation practice is probably not really teaching very much. On the other hand, oral practices of the kind discussed in detail in Chapter 10 are lively, involve everybody, and can be great fun.

It is essential to remember that you are not really trying to improve the students pronunciation – even if they think you are. You use the kind of speaking practice in Chapter 10 to bring everybody together after a period of the lesson when they have all been doing different things, to release tension if, for example, a particular student has become embarrassed in the middle of trying to say something and has got tied up in a pronunciation mistake, or simply to liven up the lesson from a rather dead period.

Take the trouble to look carefully at Chapter 10 before you teach any of your classes – particularly if the students are aged thirteen or younger – and make sure you know how to do simple speaking practice where you prompt and the whole class responds. Having this technique at your disposal will increase your confidence and competence, and provide you with a way of livening up even the dullest classes – don't underestimate it!

Chapter 8   More formal lessons

Sometimes assistants find themselves without much choice about what they should do or how they should do it. They occasionally have to take formal lessons or try their hands at normal language teaching lessons or evening groups.

Questions

The basic technique for all more formal lessons is the teacher's skill in asking and balancing different kinds of questions. The three most important types are:
- Comprehension questions
- Quotation questions
- Conversation questions

Comprehension questions

These are supposed to test the students' understanding of a text, but very often the questions that teachers ask after reading a text hardly check understanding at all. Look at this sentence and the questions and answers that follow it:

The doodlebing thrang up the hill.

> T: Well, now let's have a few questions.
>   What did the doodlebing do?
> S1: Thrang up the hill.
> T: Good. Where did it thring?
> S2: Up the hill.
> T: Good. What thrang up the hill?
> S3: The doodlebing.
> T: Good, yes. And how did it go?
> S4: It thrang.
> T: Good. Can you give me the principal parts?
> S5: Thring, thrang, thrung.
> T: Good. Now do you think it was tired when it got to the top?
> S: ???

Only the last question was a true comprehension question in the sense that it tested whether the class understood what they had read. The answers to all the other questions can be found in the text. The students who answered those questions either read the answers or made a very simple manipulation. This proved that they knew something about the basic structure of English (*What thrang up the hill?* – the answer will be the first words of the sentence, the subject).

So in asking questions about a text there will be three kinds:
1   Easy questions where the answer can be read directly from the text.
2   More difficult questions where the answer is a manipulation of the grammar of the text.
3   Much more difficult external questions which really test understanding, and where students have to understand how the words of the text relate to something outside the text.

The easiest way to construct questions is to ask questions that expect the answer 'No'. The question is based on a false assumption. For example:

Mr Brown usually gets up at seven o'clock. He has breakfast with his wife and then he goes to work. He usually goes on the bus but this week he's taking his car.

What time does he get up?
The answer can be read.

How does he usually go to work?
Again the answer can be read – but note the students should say only *On the bus*, not the full sentence.

Does he usually have breakfast on his own?
A real comprehension question.
Does he always go on the bus?
Another real comprehension question. Notice the answers start *No…*

It is important if you are doing a text or dialogue intensively to ask all three kinds of questions – but remember the first two simply practise the language of the text or dialogue and only the third kind tests understanding.

Quotation questions

Very often with a text we do not want the students to read the answers to questions (type 1 above), but if we are doing a dialogue the opposite is often true. We want them to find the exact words which are used to say something in natural English. Look at this dialogue and the questions the teacher asks about it:

A: *Would you like to come to a party on Saturday?*
B: *Oh, that'd be marvellous, but I'm afraid I can't. I'm going to see my grandmother.*

T: What does the girl say when she wants to invite her friend to the party?
S1: Do you want to come to a party?
T: No. That's what it means, but we don't usually say that. What did she say – what were her exact words?
S2: 'Would you like to come to a party'?
T: That's right … '*Would you like to …*'

Notice these questions have a double purpose. They make sure that the student really has found the exact words to make a correct natural English expression, and the teacher's first question has also provided an explanation.

The explanation here is not what it means, but why she said it. If the student has provided the words the girl uses to invite her friend, clearly the student has already understood what the phrase means. It isn't necessary to break it down into its grammatical parts, or to give a long explanation yourself.

If you are doing dialogues it's important to remember that if the students are used to texts, they are used to producing content when the teacher asks questions afterwards. When you are asking quotation questions you want the exact language that was used. It may take a while for students to get used to this. In the example above we suggest the teacher's response when the student gives the meaning but not the exact words.

Conversation questions

If the class has a good teacher, that teacher probably asks a few questions from time to time which appear more personal: 'What did you do at the weekend? Did you see … on TV last night? Have you been to…? Would you like to…? Are you interested in…?' Very often, however, the teacher's questions practise a structure or phrase which the students have just learned (past simple, *interested in*, and so on). For this reason these conversations usually only last two or three lines. Conversation questions are best used interspersed with comprehension questions:

   T: What time does Mr Brown usually get up?
   S1: Seven o'clock.
   T: That's right. What about you?
   S1: Er, about eight o'clock.
   T: Oh I see, later than Mr Brown. What about on Saturdays?
   S1: Oh, nine o'clock perhaps.
   T: (to another student) What about you?
   S2: About nine o'clock as well.
   T: But not during the week.
   S2: No, about half-past seven.
   T: I see, and you?
   S3: The same, about half-past seven.
   T: Yes, and what about Mr Brown, what does he do then?

This is a very simple text and question sequence, but the principle can be used at all levels. Don't separate conversation into a part of the lesson. Make it an integral part of some other activity. A series of short diversions is both more natural and more effective than an attempt at a long conversation session at one time.

Using a text intensively

Summary of method
1 Introduction of content and method.
2 Pre-questions.
3 Presentation by teacher or previously prepared by students.
4 Check students understand gist.
5 Check comprehension.
6 Exploit vocabulary and grammar.
7 Exploit the content.

1 Introduce the material

This means two things – give a two or three line summary of the content:

> *We're going to look at a text now about the money that's spent on the American space programme. The author talks about how much it costs and whether he thinks it's worth it or not.*

Secondly, presenting to the class how you're going to do it:

> *Close your books. I want you to listen. I'll read the text. I want you to listen especially for the answers to these two questions. Is the programme getting more or less expensive as time goes on? Does the author think the Americans should spend more or less?*

Or perhaps:

> *Follow in your books while I read. If there are any words you don't understand or you can't say put a line under them* (demonstrate) *with your pencil. We'll talk about them after I've read the text.*

The idea is to make the students active and involved during the first presentation. Don't let them read unseen round the class – they will make lots of mistakes that you feel you have to correct and the whole thing will become muddled.

2 Pre-questions

Ask some concrete comprehension questions before the first presentation of the text. This will focus attention and make the situation more natural. Usually when we are listening to someone speaking we have a good idea in advance of the sort of things they are likely to say although we do not know the details.

3 Presentation of the text

There are different ways of doing this. The least successful is reading unseen round the class. The alternatives are:

- The teacher reads – perhaps only paragraph by paragraph at lower level, longer sections at a higher level.
- The class reads after the teacher – sentence by sentence at beginner level.
- An individual student reads after the teacher – sentence by sentence at lower levels or paragraph by paragraph at intermediate levels. This is better than unseen reading, as the teacher will have already presented a

model for some language which would otherwise cause difficulties. The idea is to ensure that the student who reads gets it right – it's a presentation of the text not an obstacle course.

- Individual students read prepared paragraphs. Divide the class into groups ('All the people in this line... etc.') and get different groups to prepare different bits of the text. Go round and help them, ask individual students 'Is there anything you can't say?, Can you say... please?' etc. Then, when they have all prepared their own bits, get one individual from each group to read the prepared part.
- Silent reading. Teachers often forget that if you are reading for content (you're not at the moment interested in them saying all the words of the text) this is the quickest and most natural way of presenting a text.

You should not use the same method every time. As with most other things in a classroom, variety usually means improvement, so try to use different methods for different texts.

4 Check students understand gist
It's important before trying to use the language of the text to check that the students are not completely lost. You must have had the experience yourself of reading a difficult text, looking up all the words in the dictionary, understanding all the words and still having no idea what the text was about. In order to check comprehension you should ask a couple of questions that concentrate not on the detailed language of the text but on the gist of its meaning. If students are hopelessly lost at this point, it's wiser to forget the text.

5 Check comprehension
This means using the sort of question techniques we discussed above. Try to avoid long strings of comprehension questions that only plough through the text. It's usually more effective, more natural and more fun if you intersperse comprehension and conversation questions.

6 Exploit vocabulary and grammar
You could collect together an area of vocabulary and/or do a series of exercises. Texts which have been chosen deliberately as language teaching texts usually suggest a particular exploitation. If you read the text beforehand you soon become aware of frequent use of, for example, the past progressive tense. The primary purpose of most language teaching texts is to present particular language, not to stimulate interesting discussion about the content.

7 Exploit the content
Exploit the content of the text. If students have studied the text and particularly the language in it, they will find it much easier to talk about the content. If you bear this in mind you'll realise that the dichotomy between a formal textbook lesson and a conversation lesson based on some sort of concrete material is not as great as it sometimes appears.

Using a text extensively

Texts can be used intensively and extensively or they can be used extensively only. An extensive exploitation will use the text only as a basis for conversation.

Summary of method
1 Introduce the text.
2 Ask three or four pre-questions.
3 Students read.
4 Explain any problems you anticipate (vocabulary or content).
5 Ask for any further problems.
6 Get answers to pre-questions, then use comprehension questions to lead into conversation questions and hopefully, to natural conversation.

Note that if you choose a text for extensive reading, you must use it for that, and not be tempted into asking (or even answering) questions about its detailed grammar or vocabulary.

Using a dialogue

In schools, particularly with younger and/or less able students, a dialogue has significant advantages over a text. It is usually much shorter, less complex (i.e. single extended paragraphs are relatively rare) and, from the students' point of view, more obviously useful.

You may think that dialogues look too easy. If you're willing to try lessons of this type you will quickly find that although students can understand everything in a dialogue, when they are required to reproduce it, their efforts will be very disappointing indeed. This means that when you're choosing a dialogue you should never be worried that it will be too easy – if it is, you could always add more language or alternative ways of saying things in the course of the lesson. If, on the other hand, you choose something which is too difficult you'll give yourself considerable problems. The dialogue lesson is based on the fact that the class is going to perform, not the teacher, so the material should not be beyond them.

Summary of method
1 Teacher introduces.
2 Teacher reads prepared dialogue.
3 Teacher checks comprehension.
4 Teacher re-reads if necessary.
5 Students read after the teacher.
6 Students work in pairs.
7 Drills to practice selected phrases.
8 Free situations in pairs/groups.

1 Teacher introduces

Usually an anecdote is best:

> *A friend of mine wanted to ask me to go to Cologne with him at the weekend. What do you think he said to me? Unfortunately, another friend was coming to visit me here so I couldn't go. What do you think I said?*

In this way you show that the language the students are going to learn is useful in practical situations.

2 Teacher reads prepared dialogue

The students cannot see it, and the dialogue is used first as a listening comprehension. Read it clearly at about natural speed. It's much easier for students to follow the dialogue if, as you change roles, you change voice slightly or change position. If you read in a flat, even voice it makes it very difficult to follow. Some teachers use their hands as puppets and make their hands talk to each other to show the change of roles.

3 Teacher checks comprehension

Ask the pre-questions again, then more comprehension questions (aimed at the content) and quotation questions (aimed at the language).

4 Teacher re-reads if necessary

With new pre-questions to help with difficulties that made the second reading necessary.

5 Students read after the teacher

At this point the students see the text for the first time. Different methods of reading are practical here and variety is important – teacher followed by class, phrase by phrase; teacher followed by half classes who answer each other; individual students after the teacher.

6 Students work in pairs

By now they should understand the whole dialogue and have said all the important and difficult phrases several times.

7 Drill(s) to practise selected phrases

It is best to start with very controlled drills – perhaps the students have to add a phrase to what they are given. For example:

> T: A chemist's.
> CLASS: Excuse me, I wonder if you could tell me if there's a chemist's near here please?

8 Free situations in pairs/groups

A teacher may either explain these – but this takes quite a long time – or ideally give them out to the pairs/groups on cards. Here is a typical situation to use at the end of a lesson on invitations.

> *Jill asks Richard if he would like to play tennis on Saturday.*
> *Richard will be out of town as he's going to visit his sister.*
> *Jill suggests the following Saturday. That suits Richard very well.*

Remember that even if you have practised and drilled well up to this point, students will still find the free situation extremely difficult and will make lots of mistakes. If you have a full class working together in pairs, all talking at the same time and all making mistakes, it can seem like chaos, but the students will usually feel involved and will enjoy the activity. If you have prepared the free situations well, a lot of correct language will be used and certainly more correct sentences will be said than in a more traditional question and answer based lesson. So don't worry if there are a few minutes of apparent chaos and above all don't cut out this last and most important step. Students learn to use language by actually using it – and that means mistakes and a certain amount of noise.

Writing your own dialogues

a) Dialogue content should not be limited to pure information about people, places etc. Dialogues should contain language which illustrates personality, attitudes, social relationships.

b) Material in the dialogue should be within the range of experience and interest of your class.

c) The real purpose of presenting a dialogue is to introduce or provide further practice of language items. For example, including some functional words and useful phrases is more important than presenting an exciting story.

d) Keep the dialogue short – eight to ten lines at the most. You can always lengthen it in the class, but the opposite is not true.

Using literature

You may be teaching the oldest and most able students who are reading some work of English literature from a literary point of view. If you have read and know something about the work, or are interested in any way, you may find it possible to have a discussion with them about it and get them to tell you something about a work in their own language that they have read and enjoyed. This will involve co-operation with the native teacher. You may also find that it is possible to co-operate with teachers other than the English teacher – for example, the history teacher may be doing something about England which you yourself have studied and are interested in. In the same way, if you have other interests you may find it possible to connect what you do in your classes to what is happening in your students' other lessons in some other subject. This, however, is going to be true only for those working with students at the upper end of the secondary school.

It is impossible in an introductory work of this nature to give a comprehensive methodology for dealing with literature with EFL students. If you find yourself being asked to teach literature, we suggest you first consult your host colleagues to discover their expectations of you, as approaches to literature vary from one educational system to another.

Chapter 9   Choosing materials

Selection criteria

Starting a conversation from nothing is extremely difficult. Some local incident or something that has happened to a particular student will occasionally spark off a spontaneous discussion or conversation. Almost always, however, it is better to start from something concrete. This may be a text, video, picture, tape, anecdote told by the teacher, or whatever. The important thing is that there is some concrete focus as a basis for the conversation. You have probably already thought of using newspaper articles, pop or folk songs, maps and pictures of your country, and so on. But all too often the fascinating article from the newspaper that you have chosen for your class turns out to be a flop – which could have been predicted in advance. An article that interests you will often be linguistically or intellectually way beyond the ordinary school student, and your students will have very different interests and experiences from your own. Most assistants in the past have used the criterion 'is the subject matter interesting?' Lots of materials that pass this test for you, simply do not work in the classroom, so it is worthwhile thinking of a more comprehensive list of selection criteria.

Practical considerations

Start by considering whether the material you have in mind is practically possible in a particular situation. As soon as you arrive at your school find out about the equipment, copying facilities etc. Will you be allowed to use them? How much notice do you need to give if you want copies? Is there an overhead projector in the classroom? If so, does it have a roll of film and pens, or will you need to take your own pens? Does it have film you can take away and prepare in advance? What English newspapers and magazines does the school take? Do the other teachers use them? Use this list to check the practicality of a particular idea or a piece of material.

1 Who needs the material?
Will you need a single copy or one for each person? The practical difficulties – if there are not enough legible copies – will overwhelm everything else.

2 Is the material versatile?
Can it be used at different levels with different groups? A simple street map is a good example. A good one for use at a basic level will have a central area with right-angled street corners to practise 'finding the way'. Away from the centre it will have a roundabout and perhaps a Y-junction so that it can be used at higher levels too (e.g. 'Bear left at the traffic lights'). The map is even better if the names of different buildings are marked so that it can be used for vocabulary and perhaps even as a basis for a story ('You're standing outside the bank: What can you see? Who can you see? What's she doing? Where are they going?').

3 How long will it take to present the material?

If it is material only the teacher has, think of the following problems: How long will it take to write on the board? Can you write it on the board before the class arrives? If you are going to write on the board for more than half a minute, what are the students going to do while you are writing? If you do not give them something definite to do, they will almost certainly have ideas of their own! If you are going to read to the class, how long will that take? If more than two or three minutes, how can you break up that time? If you are going to play a tape how long will that take? Very few classes can listen to a tape of any sort for more than 90 seconds without a break. This means that you will lose the concentration of almost everybody if you play a song – they are nearly always longer than 90 seconds. If you want to avoid losing everybody's concentration you should break tapes, no matter how interesting, into short sections by, for example, asking a couple of questions or commenting yourself. In the case of material which the students also have, how long will it take them to read and understand it? How long will you spend actually using it? Materials which are to be used for conversation lessons should take a relatively short time to present. So an interesting newspaper item which takes so long to present that there is no time left to talk about it is obviously unsatisfactory. For this reason it is often better to present texts not by giving the students copies but by reading extracts yourself or even preparing a summary. If the material is to be used as the basis for a conversation or discussion, it is sufficient to summarise the main ideas.

4 How difficult is the material?

Material should be too easy rather than too difficult – difficult material invariably takes much too long to present. However, it is very easy to increase the difficulty of simple material by adding to it. In contrast, it is very difficult indeed to simplify something that was intrinsically too difficult. The material can be difficult for two different reasons   the language used to present it is intrinsically difficult, or the class does not have the background to understand it. It is not new words or expressions which make language material difficult; it is the proportion of the whole which you do not know. This is particularly important in the case of newspapers. Quality English newspapers are written at a vocabulary level of about 20,000 words. Not many learners of English have a vocabulary of even half that size. Furthermore, many words which are common in newspaper English are very uncommon in school textbooks, or in everyday spoken English. This means students will have considerable difficulty making any sense of most newspaper articles. Students will find material difficult which is outside their experience. Many will have had very little experience outside their own families and schools. Probably very few will have had experience outside their own country, except what they may have gathered from TV, so the subjects you choose and the way you handle them should reflect this. It is not very realistic to expect them to do something in a foreign language which they would find difficult even in their own.

Finally, if you expect behaviour from the students which is very different from that which they are used to in school, they will find the change difficult. In particular, if they are used to sitting quietly and reading or writing and you expect them to talk a lot, you will find it helpful to make that explicit.

5 Is the material interesting?

Nothing which is too difficult and which cannot be understood is interesting, so keep materials simple and within the students' range of experience. Here is a checklist which attempts to define more explicitly the meaning of 'interesting' in this context.

Students' considerations

1 Will it be useful to the students?

Students may feel material is useful in three contexts: for an examination; practical use when, for example, visiting England; or for their other studies. This last may require some explanation. For older students, if you can find English articles relevant to their other lessons it can be stimulating and rewarding for them and you to use these. This is relatively straightforward for English or history. In the case of science subjects where you will not have such a detailed knowledge you may find it better to use more general articles from, for example, *The Scientific American* or *The New Scientist*.

2 Does it stimulate their curiosity?

You will surely have watched a television programme on a subject which you were not interested in beforehand but which caught your imagination. This happens in class too, so you should not try to predict too certainly in advance what subjects students find interesting. Your lively presentation of the subjects you are interested in will almost certainly get them involved too. Especially useful in this respect are puzzles. The answer to the puzzle is unimportant but, well presented, most people do enjoy solving them. In Chapter 11 we suggest lots of language puzzles which exploit both the intrinsic interest of language and the intellectual challenge of puzzles or problem solving.

3 Is the material relevant to the class and individual?

Few school students will be interested in the English legal system or the industries of Yorkshire. On the other hand, two people will usually be of particular interest – the students and you. For this reason you should not be afraid to talk about yourself. If asked to do lessons about, for example, the English legal system, try to do it from a personal point of view. In the same way elicit personal responses from your students – not from one individual but from several. They will usually also be interested in information about themselves, their town and country as they are seen by other people. If you can find articles in English about their country, or the school system, or whatever, they will usually want to read these. Most importantly, what will make them most active is if the attitudes expressed in the material are surprising to them or, even better, if the factual information given is actually wrong, or prejudiced. If they believe you are misinformed, they will naturally and automatically want to correct you. The interest which arises here is no longer in the subject matter but to do with you as a person. In the same way, any matter upon which they are better informed than you will usually stimulate language. It may mean asking them about the town they live in, or getting them to explain how the tape-recorder in the classroom works. Natural conversation often depends upon an information-gap – the participants having different information at their

52

disposal. Traditional conversation lessons frequently fail precisely because everybody has the same information (the text). Much of the material we suggest exploits this information-gap, but best of all is to exploit natural situations which actually arise in the classroom.

4 Is it fun to do?

Interest frequently derives not from what is done but from how it is done. Grammar practices of the kind you probably remember yourself (*put du, de la or des in the following sentences*, followed by a seemingly endless written exercise) were usually not fun. But some of the speaking activities in Chapter 10, done quickly, can be entertaining and a few mistakes often make them both more useful and more fun.

5 Will it seem worth doing to the students?

Learners need to see the point in doing something. This is particularly true of games. Just playing games can easily seem childish, so if you do play games show *why* you played the game. Explain explicitly why you did it and what students have learned or practised.

Your considerations

Can you handle the material?

No matter how good an idea, in the end it is you, the individual teacher, who has to handle it. Bear in mind the two following points:

- Do not tackle any subjects that you don't know about. This means you should not be afraid to refuse requests like 'Could you tell them a little bit about the English legal system please?' It is not reasonable to ask you to teach what you yourself imperfectly understand.
- Do not take material into the room before you are clear what you are going to do with it. Few materials are intrinsically interesting – they depend on your exploiting them. The central question to help you decide how to handle a piece of material is, 'What linguistic activity will this generate?' This is so important we give an example. Can you think of a simple well-known game which you could play with young children which would teach them these items: *please, I'd like, have got?*
  The answer is 'Happy Families'. This is a much better conversation lesson with a class of youngsters who know very little English than a laborious effort to make them produce one or two spontaneous sentences. Many learners of English use *have* instead of *have got*, the use of *please* is also difficult for a lot of students, and they are often taught to say *I want* instead of *I'd like*. So the game we've suggested is a real significant step in the right direction for a good conversation lesson.

In summary, in the classes you give, you should not try to produce stimulating, lively discussions – of course you hope for that sometimes with some of your classes – but your general objective should be a more down-to-earth one; to produce linguistic activity in the classroom by trying to make the student talk as much as possible in a relatively controlled way.

Chapter 10 Materials 1: *Speaking practice*

Speech work can cover many things in addition to the pronunciation of individual sounds. The materials and methods which follow cover pronunciation, stress and intonation.

The following phonetic symbols are used in this section:

/ ə /	as in *ago, colour, furniture*
/ ɪ /	as in *sit*
/ iː /	as in *seat*
/ æ /	as in *sat*
/ ʌ /	as in *such*
/ θ /	as in *think*
/ ð /	as in *there*
/ ʃ /	as in *ship, sugar, nation*
/ ʒ /	as in *pleasure*
/ tʃ /	as in *church*
/ z /	as in *these, zoo*
/ j /	as in *yellow, yes*
/ dʒ /	as in *major, June*

The other letters have the normal English values (*p, b, v* etc.)

Pronunciation

Even if you will not normally be required to formally teach pronunciation, you will be expected to correct errors and help individuals with particular problems. Pronunciation is popular and useful for younger children who often have a good ability to mimic until about thirteen years old. On the other hand, for older students, bad pronunciation is often an ingrained habit and something of an embarrassment, and pronunciation teaching can be of doubtful value for such classes. Pronunciation practice activities are, however, very useful as a means of control, since they involve the whole group doing the same thing at the same time. Just remember, five minutes pronunciation work at any one time is enough.

You can do pronunciation practice:
- When someone makes a mistake which you recognise as relatively common, and therefore worth the attention of the whole class.
- When you decide to have a change of activity or pace for five minutes in the middle of the lesson.
- At the end of a lesson as a filler to give some practice on a common problem.

Materials for the pronunciation of common problem sounds

It is very easy to make your own materials for pronunciation practice. Make a list of all the sounds of English which your students find difficult. Then write some short phrases containing the sound. For example, if they find the difference between / s / and / ∫ / difficult, they will find the following phrases a problem: *She's sure. Simon's shirt. Show Sue your new silk shirt.*

They are not 'tongue twisters' in the normal sense. To use them:
1   Say them clearly yourself.
2   Write them on the board.
3   Get the whole class to repeat them after you.
4   Ask individuals to say them.

This is a light-hearted way to check up on pronunciation, and a fun thing to do for the last five minutes of a lesson. These exercises should be done quickly and in a light-hearted way. Mistakes are part of the fun, so don't expect too high a standard. It is best to do them with whole-class responses like this:

T: Cherry is going to China in March.
C: Cherry is going to China in March.
T: John...
C: John is going to China in March.
T: July...
C: John is going to China in July.
T: Germany...
C: John is going to Germany in July.

Practice materials

Sound: / dʒ /
Key words: *jacket, dangerous, large* (initial, medial and terminal positions)
Words: *jump, job, joke, German, January, age, change, damaged, passenger*

Contrast with / t∫ /
jeep – cheap   Jane – chain   Joyce – choice   jeered – cheered
joke – choke   ridge – rich   German – chairman

Contrast with / j /
jet – yet   jot – yacht   jaw – your

Phrases
In June and July.
Not just yet.
Jill's job makes Charles jealous.
George is changing his job again.
You must be joking!
Which job would you choose?

Articulation practice sentences
I like marmalade.
(enjoy – jam – John)
Charles is starting his job in July.
(John – changing – June)
The French officer had a big car.
(large – general – German)
Jill had to change planes in Manchester.
(Geneva – the children – jets)
The talk was jeered by the French workers.
(speech – cheered – German – teachers)

Sound: / ʃ /
Key words: *ship, station, Spanish*
Words: *shirt, shoes, sugar, sure, should, delicious, machine, demonstration, French*

Contrast with / tʃ /
sheep – cheap   *shoes – choose*   *shop – chop*   *wash – watch*
wish – witch   *cash – catch*

Contrast with / s /
she – see   *sheets – seats*   *shave – save*   *fashion – fasten*
push – puss

Phrases
Fish and chips.
Fashions change.
Sugar's cheap.
I'm sure she's the French tennis champion.
Some delicious Swiss chocolate.
Is this the switch?
I was so sure those were Sue's shoes.
That sort of person is never ashamed so she needs a short, sharp shock.

Articulation practice sentences
He bought an expensive car.
(cheap – chose – Charles)
This shop sells special food.
(butcher – cheap – chops)
She saw the boys running after the dog.
(chase – children – watch)
Sam got to the station before Sue.
(beach – reached – Charles)
Sarah's so funny when she speaks French.
(Shirley – Swedish – shy)

Sound: / θ /
Key words: *thank you, method, month*
Words: *think, theatre, thirsty, Thursday, nothing, birthday, author, bath, south, growth*

Contrast with / t /

thin – tin	*three – tree*	*thanks – tanks*	*thought – taught*

Contrast with / f /

three – free	*thirst – first*	*thought – fought*	*thrill – frill*

Contrast with / s /

think – sink	*thick – sick*	*thought – sought*	*thumb – some*
theme – seem	*teeth – tease*	*forth – force*	*worth – worse*

Phrases

North and south.   *They're thought to be free.*
Thirty-three.   *I think Thursday's the third this year.*
Six months.   *There were between thirty and forty there.*
Through thick and thin.   *I think I'll get them something for their birthdays.*
They fought to be free.

Articulation practice sentences

She has two showers a week.   *(Judith – bath – Thursday)*
(baths – three – month)   *He said he'd go to the cinema.*
Ethel had a swim on Tuesday.   *(theatre – thought – Mr Smith)*

Sound: / ð /
This sound is very common, as it is the initial sound of a number of important English structure words.
Key words: *then, father, with*
Words: *the, this, that, these, those, their, they, there, then, though*

It also occurs in the middle and at the end of a number of other common words. Here are some of the most important: *either, father, another, together, rather, rhythm, smooth*

Contrast with / d /

they – day	*there – dare*	*those – doze*

Contrast with / s / or / z /

though – sew	*they – say*	*that – sat*	*these – seize*	*breathe – breeze*

Phrases
This and that.
Then and there.
They're over there.
That's the brother.
This is theirs.
My mother, father and brother were there.

Articulation practice sentences
Brown's is the best café in the eastern region.
(that's – bathing place – southern)
He went to Spain yesterday.
(they – there – then)
There's a very nice plastic one there.
(another – rather – leather)

Here are some examples which combine / θ / and / ð /.
He said the situation would get worse.
(they – thought – weather)
We speak like that here.
(think – there – they)
This is for my brother's party.
(birthday – father – that)

Sound: / z /
Key words: *zoo, lazy, please*
Words: *zip, easy, busy, noisy, husband, noise, cause*
This sound is common in a number of important structural words:
is, isn't, does, these, those, his, hers, theirs, as, has
It is also needed for the pronunciation of plurals (see below).

Contrast with / s /

pens – pence	*prize – price*	*plays – place*	*knees – niece*
peas – piece	*please – police*		

Phrases Articulation practice sentences
He's lazy. *I'm annoyed by silly children.*
The summer season. *(lazy – teachers – students)*
It wasn't hers. *He has lots of property.*
His shoes. *(owns – houses – hundreds)*
It's theirs, not yours. *We gave Mary some flowers.*
Whose shoes are those? *roses – a dozen – Susan)*
Socialism is based on optimism.

Sound: / h /
Key words: *hat, behind* (does not occur in the terminal position)
This sound is mostly a problem in the initial position. Words with / h / in the middle are relatively uncommon.
Words: *half, hand, head, hear, heavy, high, home, horse, house, hundred, behind, anyhow, rehearse, perhaps, unhappy*

Contrast initial / h / and unaspirated equivalent:

hand – and	*hear – ear*	*hold – old*	*high – I*
hair – air	*hill – ill*	*heart – art*	

Phrases
He's unhappy.
Awfully heavy.
We all hurried home.
I asked her how she heard.
How awful, how did it happen?

Note: It is normal for educated speakers to drop the / h / and elide the word with the previous word, providing it is an unstressed structural word. This is not regarded as wrong and, while teaching students to aspirate words like *hand, head, hotel,* they must be taught at the same time to make elisions in phrases like 'He must've had his hair cut' or 'It's not his own'.

Articulation practice sentences
John had a wonderful trip.
(Harry – awful – holiday)
He was the most popular person in the film.
(actor – handsome – Hollywood)

Sound: / w /
Key words: *window, sandwich* (does not occur in the final position)
Words: This sound is common at the beginning of a number of important structural words: *when, which, what, why, were, where, was, one, well, will, with*
Other common words: *whether, watch, wonderful, water, way, woman, always, between, question, twelve, twenty, twice, everywhere, quiet*

Contrast with / v /

wet – vet	*wire – via*	*west – vest*	*wine – vine*
wheel – veal	*worse – verse*	*wail – vale*	

Phrases
Very well, thank you.
A wonderful view over the water.
World War One.
We're having a holiday in November.
Why are you going away in winter?
We always go to warmer weather in winter.
Well, will the weather be very warm then?

Articulation practice sentences
They had terrible trouble.
(weather – we – wonderful)
They were asking where it happened.
(wonder – when – we)
There's a marvellous view of the lake from our garden.
(water – window – wonderful)

Sound: / ɪ /
Key words: *sit, minute, beginning*
Words: *ill, film, interesting, fifty, recipe, publicity*

Contrast between / ɪ / and / iː /
ship – sheep	*it – eat*	*sit – seat*	*his – he's*
filled – field	*pitch – peach*	*bitten – beaten*	

Phrases
Fifty minutes.
At the beginning of the film.
If he's ill he needs some pills.
A cheap tin of peas.
He hit the dog that bit him with a stick.
I hope you're not being greedy, filling it so full!

Pronouncing plurals, third-person present simple, and regular past tenses

Plurals

Most English words make their plural form by adding *-s* to the spelling, but there are three different ways of pronouncing this final *-s*:

After a voiceless sound: / s /
books, hats
After a voiced sound: / z /
plays, bottles
After / ʃ / / s / / z / / ʒ / / tʃ / or / dʒ / : / ɪz /
buses, garages

Third-person present simple

The same rules apply here. There are three different ways of pronouncing the final *-s* depending not upon the preceding letter but upon the preceding sound: / s / *walks* / z / *plays* / ɪz / *rushes*

Regular past tense

Again, although the spelling is always *-ed*, there are three different ways of pronouncing it:

After a voiceless sound: / t /
smoked, watched
After a voiced sound: / d /
slowed, opened
After / t / or / d /: / ɪd /
visited, handed

Here is a list of regular verbs. You may want to use it to help students practise the three different pronunciations of *-ed*.

annoyed	guessed	worked	slowed
liked	listened	decided	cleaned
ruined	suggested	visited	missed
suited	booked	opened	looked
cooked	shouted	smoked	knocked
sounded	closed	handed	phoned
smiled	pulled	enjoyed	waited
hated	raced	remembered	called
danced	baked	passed	played
needed	allowed	wanted	laughed

When you are doing simple drills with students which involve them making plural forms or third-person present simple forms they may have trouble with the pronunciation of the *-s* ending. If so, explain that there are three different ways of pronouncing it and then get them to practise making the regular forms in the same way as you can do with these past tense forms.

The most common sound in English

The most common vowel sound in English is / ə /. Most European learners over-pronounce it, usually using the obvious vowel from the spelling. Students should be encouraged to say words naturally and to reduce the vowel to / ə /. It can replace many different letters or groups of letters. Here is a list of words where the underlined letters are pronounced / ə /.

alarm	pict<u>ure</u>	sal<u>a</u>d	m<u>a</u>chine
<u>a</u>nnoy	long<u>er</u>	p<u>o</u>lite	t<u>o</u>mato
<u>o</u>bey	oper<u>a</u>	p<u>er</u>haps	terrible
<u>o</u>ffence	sulph<u>ur</u>	b<u>a</u>n<u>a</u>n<u>a</u>	pil<u>o</u>t
doct<u>or</u>	coll<u>a</u>r	am<u>ateur</u>	glam<u>orous</u>
c<u>o</u>l<u>ou</u>r	chauff<u>eur</u>	condit<u>ion</u>	c<u>ou</u>rag<u>eous</u>

There are a large number of structural words in English that have (at least) two forms – one strong and one weak. The use of weak forms is an essential part of English, and English spoken only with the full strong forms sounds strange or even wrong. You should look for the following words that may be given their strong form mistakenly. Encourage students to produce weak forms whenever they are speaking. Here are the words normally reduced by native speakers when unstressed:

and	his	are	can	at	as	her	be	shall
for	but	them	is	will	from	than	us	was
a	of	that	do	has	an	to	he	does
have	the	not	him	am	had	some		

Here are some phrases and sentences that contain a lot of reduced words. Use one or two of the phrases from time to time to remind students how important the / ə / sound and the weak forms of the structural words are.

In a week or two.   *How nice, we'd love to.*   *Shall we ask him to help?*
I come from London.   *John and George.*   *Who am I speaking to, please?*
What was that?   *He gave her some.*   *When could we come?*
As soon as possible.   *That'll be all, thank you.*   *Where are we going?*
He's left his hat.   *It's old, but I like it.*   *Did you tell me?*

Here are some longer sentences:

At least it wasn't as bad as he'd thought.
He's just been to the dentist's and had his teeth out.
Of course I could've done it, if I'd had to.
Does he want to give her some of them?
Shall I take her to the hospital? Or do you want to?
You must do what the doctor says or you'll get worse.

Stress and emphasis

Certain phrases, particularly initials and phrases like *boy scout* where the two-word phrase is made of words which can stand independently, usually take an even, regular stress. Here are some practice materials.

Say these:

1 ABC	6 UN	11 GMT	16 PR
2 BBC	7 TV	12 ICI	17 VIP
3 SOS	8 CIA	13 KLM	18 TUC
4 IRA	9 CBI	14 USA	19 MP
5 IBM	10 FBI	15 EC	20 RIP

Say the following phrases, and stress all the words.
1   front room
2   second-hand
3   New Year
4   boy scout
5   Red Cross
6   bathroom door
7   left-hand drive
8   ballpoint pen
9   First World War
10 Second World War
11 I'm thinking of taking on a part-time job.
12 I'm getting a part-time job at weekends in the New Year.
13 My friend has just bought a second-hand sports car.
14 My friend has just bought a left-hand-drive, second-hand sports car.

Practise saying these sentences with a strong stress on the word in bold.

1   I expect to arrive about **seven** o'clock.
2   **I** expect to arrive about seven o'clock.
3   I **expect** to arrive about seven o'clock.

4   My husband's going to a **conference** next week.
5   My husband's going to a conference **next** week.
6   My **husband's** going to a conference next week.

7   There are **too** many tourists in London.
8   There are too many **tourists** in London.
9   There are too many tourists in **London.**

Form different questions by changing the stress on these questions so that you will get the answers given:

1   Is John going to Germany in June?
   a) No, Mary is.
   b) No, he's going to Switzerland.
   c) No, he's going in July.

2   Is Maria going to be chair of the meeting?
   a) No, she's going to be the secretary.
   b) No, she's going to be chair on Thursday.
   c) No, James is.

3   Did Richard take the children to the pictures
   a) No, he went alone.
   b) No, Charles did.
   c) No, he took them to the beach.

4   Did you say you were going to Paris tomorrow for a fortnight?
   a) No, to Rome.
   b) No, for a week.
   c) No, the day after tomorrow.

5   Is your son going by air to Paris?
   a) No, my daughter is.
   b) No, he's going by train.
   c) No, he's going to Berlin.

The final stress practice can be done using a quick sketch with pin figures on the board.
Where's your mother?   *She's downstairs.*
(*down stairs* – said with even stress on both words)

*Is your mother upstairs?   No, she's **down**stairs*
(said with extra stress on *down*)

In an open question like 'Where's your mother?' the answer 'She's downstairs' will have even stress on *down* and *stairs*. If the answer to the question corrects something in the question, extra stress will be given to the correction.

Intonation

How you say something can sometimes – particularly with one word or a short phrase – be more important than what you say.

Say these examples, making a clear difference between the two different kinds of question.

1	Bread?	5	Soup or fruit juice?
2	Butter?	6	Fish or meat?
3	Salt and pepper?	7	Boiled potatoes or chips?
4	Mustard?	8	Beer or wine?

Say these words and phrases as questions.

1	Twelve?	6	Ten pounds?	11	Fifty?
2	Spain?	7	Six o'clock?	12	This evening?
3	By car?	8	Jill?	13	At Christmas?
4	Next week?	9	Your mother?	14	Three weeks?
5	A month?	10	Yesterday?	15	London?

Now practise in pairs using the following:
  A: Tomorrow? (as a suggestion/question)
  B: Tomorrow! (surprise at the suggestion)

Show doubt, enthusiasm, and surprise by saying the following:

1	Yes.	3	I see.	5	Of course.	7	Really.
2	Thank you.	4	Oh.	6	Certainly.	8	Mmmm.

Use these dialogues to show surprise, doubt, and enthusiasm:

Surprise
1 A: I met Prince Philip today
   B: Prince Philip!
2 A: I'm going to Africa next week
   B: Africa!

Doubt
1 A: I'm sure that was Prince Philip
   B: Prince Philip …
2 A: You've always wanted to go to Africa, haven't you?
   B: Africa …

Enthusiasm
1 A: Is there anyone you'd like to meet?
   B: Prince Philip!
2 A: Where shall we go next year?
   B: Africa!

Here are some more prompts:
The Queen, China, The President, Moscow, Princess Diana, South America, Michael Jackson, Iceland, Madonna, on Concorde, Boris Becker

Encourage the other person to speak using these patterns:

A: I've just been to Italy.
B: Really?

A: I've just been to Italy.
B: Italy?

A: I've just been to Italy.
B: Have you?

Practise in pairs (using all three responses above) with the following:
1 I haven't seen Bill for ages.
2 Switzerland was a bit dull.
3 She's just passed her driving test.
4 She's getting married.
5 He's a famous actor.
6 It's pretty expensive.
7 She's just bought a moped.
8 He was really annoyed.
9 I had a fight with him.
10 We were at school together.
11 They've got a lovely house.
12 She's going to England.
13 It wasn't a very good game.
14 I bought it in London.
15 I'm playing tennis on Saturday.
16 I can't find my pen anywhere.

Simple oral drills

Grammar practice probably conjures up in your own mind written work and endless gap-fill exercises from your school-days. In contrast to that drudgery, the oral drill is much more entertaining.

Simple oral drills are particularly worthwhile if you have less able or younger students where having a conversation is impossible, because it involves everybody and means many students get to speak a lot of correct English. In addition, if your classes are quiet and unresponsive, you can use oral practice to bring them to life and make everyone active. Silence or only one person speaking can be boring.

The practice is best done teacher to class – you give a prompt and the whole class gives the response. Take a simple grammar point and make the class change a sentence quickly by inserting a new element given by the teacher. From a practical point of view the drills are not as simple as they look. The first time you try it, it's easiest to write the first few steps on the board to show the students what they are expected to do. Having done that, you can go on to use the idea again and again, since the students know what is expected of them. The teacher needs a slip of paper or a card with the prompts, and a board to write up the first few examples to give the class the pattern. The practice depends on the speed with which you do it. The whole idea is that students respond automatically.

Notice how little the teacher says in these drills, giving the prompts and no more. If the drill breaks down or the students get lost, no explanation is needed; just go back one step to an example they did correctly. In all of these drills it's important that the teacher has worked out the prompts before the lesson – it's best to have made a list of them, for example, on a library card so that you can keep the prompts before you while doing the drill.

Aim: third person -*s: He likes tea.*	Aim: *So … I Neither … I*
T: Repeat: I like coffee.	T: I like cheese.
C: I like coffee.	C: So do I.
T: We…	T: I can swim.
C: We like coffee.	C: So can I.
T: Tea…	T: I'm going swimming.
C: We like tea.	C: So am I.
T: He…	T: I can't play tennis.
C: He likes tea.	C: Neither can I.
T: Hate…	T: I don't know Mary very well.
C: He hates tea.	C: Neither do I.
T: My mother…	
C: My mother hates tea.	
T: My parents…	
C: My parents hate tea.	
T: My sister…	

and so on.

Here are some language areas which lend themselves to the kind of drilling we have just mentioned.

1	third person -*s*	I *live* at home. He *lives* at home.
2	*Many* used with countable nouns *Much* used with uncountables, i.e. nouns we do not see as units	How $\begin{matrix}\textit{much}\text{ money}\\\textit{many}\text{ apples}\end{matrix}$ have you got? I haven't got $\begin{matrix}\textit{much}\text{ time.}\\\textit{many}\text{ friends.}\end{matrix}$
3	Formation of (regular) adverbs by adding -*ly* to the adjective	He's a *dangerous* driver. He drives *dangerously.*
4	Difference between past simple (*saw*) and present perfect (*have seen*)	I*'ve* just *seen* Rachel. Oh, *have* you? I *saw* her yesterday.
5	Regular comparative adjectives and those requiring *more*	She's *taller* than I am. She's *more intelligent* than me.

6   Countries, adjectives and languages

He's from *Italy*.
Yes, he's *Italian*.
Of course, he speaks *Italian*.

7   Adding the tag to a statement

They're married.
They're married, *aren't they?*

8   Possessive adjectives: *mine, yours,*
his, hers, ours, its, theirs,
Mary's, the Smiths'

It belongs to me – it's *mine*
It belongs to Sarah – it's *Sarah's*.

9   Making negatives with *do*

I like coffee.
I *don't* like coffee.

The main problems for speakers of other languages

French native-speakers

Each syllable in French has approximately the same length and stress. French rhythm is based on an equal number of stresses in each time unit. English rhythm is based on an equal number of stressed syllables in each time unit. To achieve this, English reduces a great many intervening syllables. Many English structural words (auxiliary verbs, pronouns etc.) are most often produced with weak forms. These do not exist in French and cause considerable problems since students usually over-pronounce. This means that / ə / is usually replaced by other vowels according to the spelling.

The main phonetic difficulties are as follows:
/ ɪ / and / iː / are confused. Usually / iː / is used for both.
/ æ / and / ʌ / are confused. Usually / ʌ / is used for both.
The / r / sound in French is different from its English equivalent.
/ h / does not occur in French and is often omitted in English *('e's been on 'is 'olidays)*.
/ θ / and / ð / do not occur in French and are usually replaced by / s / and / z /.

Spanish native-speakers

Rhythm in Spanish is like that of French. Usually each syllable has approximately the same length, and the grouping of syllables which occurs in English does not normally occur in Spanish. This means Spanish students usually have problems with the weak forms of unstressed words and the use of / ə / in weak syllables. / ə / is usually replaced by another vowel suggested by the spelling (with the addition of / r / if the spelling has an *r*).

Spanish has no distinction between long and short vowels, the Spanish vowels corresponding most closely to English short vowels. This makes the English long vowels a problem for the Spanish learner. In addition, the following phonetic problems are uncommon:
/ b / and / v / are often confused. Spaniards usually prefer / b /.
/ ð / and / d / are confused.
/ s / and / z / are confused, the Spanish student usually using / s / in all cases.

/ ʃ / and / ʒ / do not occur in Spanish. Both are usually replaced by / s /.
/ dʒ / and / tʃ / are usually confused, / tʃ / being used for both.
/ ʃ / is sometimes pronounced / tʃ /.

Clusters of consonants are rare in Spanish. This means that, like Italians, Spanish students have a tendency to insert a vowel sound between consonant pairs either when they occur within a word, or between two words when the first terminates with a consonant sound and the second starts with a consonant sound *('scusa me)*.

Italian native-speakers

In the same way as French and Spanish students, Italian students find weak forms of unstressed words or weak syllables, usually containing / ə / in English, difficult as such forms tend not to occur in Italian.

Almost all Italian words end in vowels. This results in a tendency to pronounce a written vowel (in words like *hide, made*) or to add a redundant vowel *(he's gota the letta)*.

Italian combinations of vowels tend always to be given their full value. As a result, Italian students find English diphthongs difficult. The following sounds, which do not occur in Italian, are likely to cause problems:

/ θ / and / ð / – they are more likely to produce / t / and / d /.
/ w / – although an approximation to this sound occurs in Italian, students often produce / v /.
/ h / – this is always silent in Italian.
/ r / – this is trilled much more emphatically in Italian.
/ ʒ / – this does not occur and will need to be practised.

German native-speakers

The difficulties for German speakers, in contrast to speakers of Romance languages, are less likely to be concerned with stress. Their main problems will be phonetic and are as follows:

/ θ / and / ð / do not occur in German. German speakers usually replace them by / s / and / z /.
/ ʒ / and / dʒ / do not occur (except in borrowed words) in German. They are usually replaced by / ʃ / and / tʃ /.
/ w / and / v / are confused, / v / being used for both. This is often a reading rather than a pronunciation problem, but attention still needs to be given to it.
/ ə / is usually over-pronounced. At the end of a word it is usually too like the English / ə /, and elsewhere in a word too close to the English / ɪ /.

Chapter 11 Materials 2: *Language games*

In our Golden Rules and basic lesson planning, we suggested that you always need to have a safety net – a number of activities which you can use for five-minute fillers either to change the pace of a lesson, or at the end of a lesson. Particularly useful in this area are language games. The key to a good language teaching game is not just fun; there should be a serious teaching or revision point. They are particularly useful for younger students, but we advise you to familiarise yourself with all of the games in this section, selecting those which you think are suitable as reserve plans for your typical classes.

Alphabet games

These games are aimed more at younger students. The basic idea is that the teacher sets a theme and then goes round the class, each student giving a word beginning with the next letter of the alphabet.

Holidays
T: I'm going on holiday to Africa.
S1: And I'm going on holiday to Bulgaria.
S2: And I'm going to China.
This then goes round the class, each student repeating the sentence with a new country. It can also be done with capital cities or names of towns.

The last letter game
The teacher starts by giving one word:
T: dangerous.
S1: silly.
S2: yacht.
And so on, the next person saying any word that comes into their head, starting with the last letter of the previous word.

Jobs
T: When I leave school I'm going to become an architect.
S1: And I'm going to become a bus driver.
And so on round the class.

Adjectives
T: On my way here I saw an awful accident.
S1: And I saw a broken down bus.
S2: I bought a cheap pair of shoes.
And so on, each student saying something that he or she did, saw, bought, etc., using an adjective beginning with the next letter.

Hangman

This is a popular game in language classes but it does generate relatively little language. You can improve it by insisting students use the phrase 'Is there … in it please?' rather than just calling out letters.

I spy

The verb *spy* is rather unusual. Change the traditional game to make it more useful in the language classroom by using, for example:, 'I've just seen something beginning with …' or 'I can see something beginning with…'

Missing letters

Write a number of words on the board with their first two letters missing. Students have to produce any word which ends with the letters you've given, for example: if you put TLAW they can add OU. This can be a good deal more difficult than you would expect. Here are some examples you may like to use:

ORT	VEL	ANGES	EW
LEEP	URCH	TROL	READY
USE	INK	TTY	ONG
OOR	UNG	OON	AIN
OWER	OTES	ILET	EEL

It's a good idea to use words that students have had trouble remembering or have had difficulty in saying in an earlier lesson.

Jumbled letters

Write on the board groups of letters with a theme, but jumble the letters of the words. Here, for example, are different kinds of animals:

EPSEH   LAHEW   RESHO   XOF   RABE   TAPLEHEN   NILO

REGIT   WCO   ORGAKONA   NEREDERI   ANESK   GFOR

MYNEKO   OGD   EMUSO

Make this activity more difficult by using adjectives or words students have learnt in an earlier lesson.

Missing vowels

The teacher writes a simple sentence on the board but omits all the vowels:

WHRDDYBYT?

CNYTLLMTHWYTTHSTTNPLS?

The students try to solve the conundrum by supplying the vowels. This activity also trains skills of association from a visual stimulus in telegraphic or abbreviated forms. It is very much easier if the word breaks and missing letter spaces are shown:

TH_R_ W_S A M_N _N TH_ G_RD_N.

It is much more of a puzzle if the word breaks are not shown:

H_V_Y_ _B_ _NT_L_ND_NB_F_R_?

Be careful with this activity, because if you use words mostly made of vowels, the problem becomes almost impossible. Avoid too many *I, a, you, our* type words.

Making words
The teacher writes a long word on the board, and individuals or groups are given a few minutes to write down as many new words as possible using only the letters of the word on the board. The group/individual with the most wins. It's best to include common letters in your word if you want to make it easier. Try, for example, *teacher, English, Christmas, stranger, television.*

Vocabulary games

What's my line?
A student volunteers to start. She or he thinks of a job and comes to the front of the class. The other students then ask questions to find out what the job is. This game generates questions in the present beginning with *do.* Before starting, the teacher must tell the class how they are to ask the questions, either round the class or by putting their hands up. Twenty-five people shouting questions at the same time is chaos. It's also a good idea with younger classes to suggest before the game starts some of the questions they might ask. For example:
Is your job usually done by a man/woman?
Do you wear a uniform of any kind?
Do you work indoors/outdoors?
Do you work alone?
Is your job a glamorous/dangerous one?
Do you use any tools?
Do you make things?
Do you need a special qualification for your job?
Do you work in a factory/office/hospital etc …?
Are you a …?

Who am I?
This is a variation on the previous game, except that the student at the front is either a famous personality from the present or from history. It is best if the teacher decides on the character and slips a piece of paper to the student with the name written on it. (Remember, people who are dead generate *did* questions.)

Other variations:
I've just been given a present, what do you think it is?
What do you think I'm going to do this weekend?
Where am I going on holiday? What did I do last night?

Twenty questions

The class asks one person questions about a mystery object decided on by the teacher. They are given some information at the beginning (*It's a place/thing* etc. for younger classes). They are then allowed twenty questions to find out what it is. Make sure the person who comes to the front of the class to answer is one of the better students.

The yes/no game

The teacher goes round the class in turn (perhaps use teams for younger students) asking rapid questions. The words *yes* and *no* are not allowed in the answer. Anyone using one of those words must drop out. This forces the use of alternative manipulative or functional answers (*I do, I have, That's right, I'm afraid you're mistaken*). The winner is the student who lasts out without using *yes* or *no*.

Hint: As questioner, repeat the answers as they are given to you, for example:

Q: What time did you get up this morning?
A: Seven o'clock
Q: Seven o'clock?
A: Yes. (A has to drop out.)

Nationalities

Give each student a card on which is written a nationality: *German, French, Japanese*, etc.). Each student has to talk a little about what she or he wears, thinks, eats, likes, and so on as if a person of that nationality. The class guesses the nationality.

Where am I?

Give each student a card on which is written the name of a place, then students talk abut the place answering these questions:
What can you see?
What can you hear?
What are the people around you doing?
For elementary groups use simple places, for example: the railway station, the cinema, etc. For more advanced groups try more difficult places such as in a submarine, etc.

What am I doing?

One student describes what she or he is doing, scoring one point for each statement made about it before the other students guess what the activity is. She or he must describe it accurately and in the proper sequence. With less able groups you may want to give them the actions on cards such as making a cup of coffee, unlocking and opening a door, packing a suitcase, and so on.

Team games

Many students, particularly younger ones, enjoy competing in teams against each other. Here are some suggestions:

Hiding and finding

This is basically a vocabulary and grammar practice game. First the teacher draws a house on the board and asks, 'I'm standing in the kitchen/hall/sitting room, what can I see?' The class supplies vocabulary items for furniture, etc. Then the class is divided into teams. The teacher says, 'I bought my mother a Christmas present and I want to hide it somewhere so she can't find it. See if you can find out where I've hidden it. Each team can ask me a question in turn but I only say *yes* or *no* and the team that guesses where the present is gets a point.'

Students may need some help with the questions which should lead towards the correct answer, for example:
Is it upstairs/downstairs?
Is it in the sitting room/kitchen/big bedroom?
It is behind/under/in/on etc, something? (to establish which preposition is appropriate).
Is it under the bed/bookcase/etc?

It's also possible to let a student 'hide' something. Different grammatical forms are possible for the question:
Did you hide it …?
Have you hidden it …?
Will you put it …?
Are you going to put it …?
The game can also be extended to 'When I was in Cairo I lost my pen' and similar variations.

Associations

The old game where someone starts with a word and the next person says the first word that comes into their head. If challenged on a word a player must be able to explain the association; for example: *aeroplane, airport, customs, passport, photograph* etc.

Suitcase game

Imagine you're going on holiday. What will you put in your suitcase?
The game goes round the class, each person giving a different thing they will take with them. It can be made more difficult by making it an alphabet game too, making all words begin with the same or consecutive letters.

Building

The teacher or one of the students says any letter. The next player has to add another, and the third another and so on; but each additional letter must be one more to the correct spelling of a word. The object of the game is to keep going as long as possible without finishing a word. Any player who finishes a word loses a life; anyone losing three lives is out of the game. All letters added must be leading to a word; if one player adds a letter which another player thinks is not building up to a word, then that player may be challenged to say what word they were thinking of. If they cannot answer they lose a life; if they give a correct word then the challenger loses a life.

Areas of vocabulary

The class is divided into teams. The teacher gives an area of vocabulary, for example: adjectives to describe people. Each team then collects words and the group with the most examples after five minutes wins. A variation is to let one member of the team write the words on the board: words that are spelt wrongly lose points.

Possible areas of vocabulary could be: food (for breakfast/lunch), the home, furniture, jobs, buildings, kinds of tree, kinds of flowers, sports, transport, names of countries etc.

Similarities and differences

The teacher writes two words on the board. For example: CAT COW
Students try to find as many features as possible that they have in common – the similarities, for example: *they are both animals, have four legs, are tame*, etc. They then suggest all the differences they can think of, such as: *the cow has horns, but not the cat, the cat can be a house pet; one is bigger than the other.* Continue with new pairs of words, working first in pairs, then checking in the whole class. Nouns are easiest, adjectives are more difficult.

Telepathy

The teacher thinks up a short, simple sentence and draws a line on the board to represent each word in the sentence (it is important to use a high proportion of structural, rather than content words, if the activity is to be effective):

____ __ _____ ___ _____ ____ ____
(Both) (my) (mother) (and) (father) (were) (there)

Students call out any word. If it is not in the sentence, ignore them completely – don't react at all or say anything. If the word is included, write it in – again without saying anything. This is difficult at the beginning but gets easier as words are added. If the students find it impossible, give them a clue – or even a word.

Notes

Each student writes a sentence in English on a small piece of paper. They turn the paper over, and write a translation into their own language on the other side. (NB: do not do this from their language into English; always start with the English sentence, which can be as easy or unusual as they like.) Students then swap papers with a partner, native language side up. The partner tries to translate into English. If the two English suggestions are the same, not really interesting; if they differ, discuss in whole class. Suitable for more advanced classes – and much more lively than it sounds here!

Tongue-twisters

A tongue-twister will always fill a few minutes, but it is better to use one based on your students' particular pronunciation problems, rather than a normal native-speaker problem. One of these, however, can always be used to amuse younger classes – *red lorry, yellow lorry*.

Introduce as follows:

> *Can you say this,* (write *red* on the board) *and this,* (put *yellow* on the board under *red*) *and this?* (put *lorry* on the board – draw it if they don't understand the word). *Now, if anyone can say 'red lorry, yellow lorry' three times without a mistake and without a pause, you can finish five minutes early.*

Result – someone can and you let them go early, or, much more likely, no one can and it takes five minutes for everyone to try!

Chapter 12 Materials 3: *Topics*

Conversation lessons

The conversation lesson built round a topic-based discussion is one of the most difficult lessons to make work. This is particularly true with younger or less able students. However, you may either be asked to do conversation lessons or want to try for yourself. Remember that your students are younger than you. Something that fascinates you may be a total turn-off for a class of fourteen year olds. This is particularly true of social issues. The average teenager is usually more interested in the latest pop video than in the problems of the homeless.

Here are some basic rules for conversation lessons:
- You must have a specific objective in mind. It's no good going in with the idea of talking about 'smoking'. There are probably at least three or four different lessons there – smoking and health, smoking and advertising, and smoking in public places. This does not mean you over-restrict students, but the more specific you are able to keep the discussion, the greater the language practice they are getting, and the more topics you will have at your disposal for later in the year.
- If you are able to take into the room something concrete such as a text or picture, you will usually find it easier to start a discussion in a natural way.
- Although not a particular topic, making the class talk about various aspects of their own country is one of the most useful themes you can use in your discussion lessons. There is little point in you telling classes about your country for the sake of it, but there is every point in doing so in order to stimulate them to talk in a similar way about their own country. You should try and use this tactic wherever possible in the following suggested topics. It is particularly applicable to topics such as food, education, social customs and behaviour, language, and all aspects of society.

Topics for conversation lessons

Host town/host country
- *What are the main attractions/industries of your town?*
- *Where would you take a visitor/definitely not take a visitor?*
- *What could be done to improve your town?*
- *Make a list of its facilities and where it is deficient.*

Draw an outline map of the country on the board. Tell the class that it is to be buried so that hundreds of years from now people will be able to dig it up and find out what their country was like. Ask different groups to mark on it three places with beautiful scenery/important industries/suitable for holidays/famous in history/famous for good food/centres for sport/old customs etc.

- ◆ *You have two American cousins coming to visit you for two weeks. You would like to show them the country. Plan a two-week trip round your country.*
- ◆ *What makes you proud to be (French etc.)? Is there anything in your country you're ashamed of? What are the main/best/worst characteristics of your compatriots?*
- ◆ *Florence is a very industrialised city isn't it?*

Making a wrong statement about the host country will very often stimulate much more discussion than a question. Students love to correct their misinformed teachers.

Hobbies
- ◆ *What hobbies do you have? How long do you spend on them? How often?*
- ◆ *Do they cost a lot? Why would you recommend your hobbies to other people?*
- ◆ *Discuss 'Hobbies should be taught in school otherwise people won't know what to do with their free time,' or 'Someone who has no hobbies does not know what life is about.'*

Sports
- ◆ *What sports do you play?*
- ◆ *Do you prefer team games or individual games?*
- ◆ *Persuade someone else in the class they should play the sports that you play.*
- ◆ *'People shouldn't worry about winning. It's enough just to take part.'*
- ◆ *Do you think that sports competitions between countries help international understanding?*
- ◆ *Did you watch the last Olympic Games? Were they political?*
- ◆ *'A huge political hoax' or 'The greatest aid to world peace.' These are two common views of the Olympics. What do you think? Do your parents agree?*
- ◆ *At the moment, sport is paid for by the people who watch it, whereas the arts are paid for very largely by state subsidies. Is this fair?*
- ◆ *'Boxing is not a sport, it's cruel.'*
- ◆ *'Gambling: sport's about doing things for fun, not making money.'*
- ◆ *'I hate sport on television – there's no atmosphere.'*
- ◆ *'It must be awful to be a professional sportsman or sportswoman having to win. Sport should be for fun.'*

The family
- ◆ *How many brothers and sisters have you got? What are they called?*
- ◆ *What do they do?*
- ◆ *What about your cousins/uncles/aunts/grandparents? Draw a family tree for your family and say a bit about everybody.*

The arts

◆ *Classical music, the opera, ballet, the theatre etc.; have you ever been to any of these? Where? When? What did you see/hear?*

◆ *Do you know anyone who never goes to any of these? What facilities are there in your town for them?*

◆ *'Opera is a minority interest, so why should the majority pay anything for it.' What do you think?*

◆ *People who live in country areas have got to pay income tax so that people in the big cities can go to ballet. Is this fair?*

◆ *Your local library – can you borrow books? Records? Listen to music at the library? What other facilities has it got?*

◆ *'The theatre is much more exciting than the cinema or television!'*

◆ *Would you like to be an actor? Why/why not?*

Age

◆ *What's your first memory?*

◆ *Can you remember your first day at school?*

◆ *Why do you remember that in particular?*

◆ *Do you believe there is a generation gap?*

◆ *Work in groups and discuss what has changed most since your parents/grandparents were your age.*

◆ *What kind of things do you disagree about most with older people? Whose fault is it?*

◆ *Do you agree or disagree with the following:*

  1 Young people should not get married before they're 21.
  2 I'd rather take my holidays with my parents.
  3 All families should spend two hours together at home every evening.
  4 Parents ought to be stricter with their children.
  5 If I had a problem I'd always go to my parents rather than my friends.
  6 Parents should let their children buy their own clothes.

◆ *What do you think is the ideal age to get married? Should people always marry people of their own age?*

◆ *'20-year-old woman marries 70-year-old man'. What do you think of that?*

◆ *What do you think is the ideal age?*

Note: With these activities it is much better to use half a dozen sentences with the 'Do you agree with these or not?' technique. It is easy to make up a further set of your own.

Clothes

◆ *Make a list of men's clothes/women's clothes (Also include types of material).*

◆ *Do you buy your own clothes?*

◆ *How do you choose your clothes – to last, or to be in fashion?*

◆ *'Fashion is just a way of wasting money.' Do you agree?*

Note: This subject is much more difficult than most people think. With lower levels it usually only consists of making a list of vocabulary. Most people find it difficult to have a discussion about clothes.

Boys and girls

◆ *Is your school mixed? Do you think it should/should not be?*

◆ *'Girls should be allowed to play football and boys should be allowed to learn cooking.' What do you think?*

◆ *Are there any jobs that only men or women should do? What are they, and why do you think that?*

◆ *'Modern girls expect too much – the same opportunities and boys to take them out, pay for them, and so on.'*

◆ *'Boys/men have more fun in life than girls/women.' Do you agree?*

◆ *'Men and women really are different – why pretend they are the same?'*

Food

◆ *What have you had to eat today? What do you normally have for breakfast/lunch/dinner?*

◆ *What's your favourite food? Which do you hate most?*

◆ *What food is your country famous for? What about the region where you live?*

◆ *Are there many restaurants in your town? Are there any foreign ones?*

◆ *Do you ever eat out? Where? Why?*

◆ *Plan your ideal meal. What would you eat? Who would you invite?*

◆ *If you're in a hurry, what do you normally make yourself to eat? Are we losing our standards of eating because of convenience foods? What food would you like to see banned?*

Relationships

◆ *How many brothers and sisters have you got? Are they your friends? Do you fight much? What about?*

◆ *What sort of people are your friends? Are they all of the same age? Are you interested in the same things? Why are they your friends?*

◆ *Do you ever read the problem page in magazines? Have you ever written to one? What kind of people write to them? What are 'typical problems'?*

Newspapers/magazines/comics

◆ *What was the last newspaper/magazine/comic that you bought? Do you buy it regularly? Why? Describe it.*

◆ *Does your town have a local newspaper? What's it like? What kind of things does it report? What kind of newspapers or magazines can you buy from your local newsagent?*

◆ *What did today's papers say? What are the most important newspapers in your country? When and where are they published? Which do your parents read? Why?*

◆ *A lot of things that get into the newspapers are not really news. What kind of thing do you think is important to read about in the newspapers? What kind of thing would you like to see disappear from newspapers?*

◆ *Are all the newspapers in your country objective? Talk about the different ones and say what their political standpoint is.*

◆ *'There won't be any newspapers in twenty years' time – just a little electronic machine in your sitting room.' Do you agree?*

Holidays

◆ *Where did you go on your last holiday? What did you do? Who went with you? What was it like? Will you go back there?*

◆ *What's important about a good holiday? Put the following in order of importance: sunshine, few people, good food, beautiful scenery, theatres, opera, swimming, museums, good shops, discos, etc.*

◆ *Work in groups of four and plan your dream holiday.*

Bicycles, mopeds and cars

◆ *Do you have a bike/moped/car? Who bought it? Do you really need it?*

◆ *'People who drive mopeds should be forced to take a driving test and wear a crash helmet all the time.' What do you think?*

◆ *Make a list of all the parts of your bike/moped in English.*

◆ *Have you done anything special to your bike/moped? How would someone know it was yours?*

◆ *'No one needs a car, but a lot of people need a status symbol.' This is a common view of why people own a car. Do you/your parents own a car? What do you/they need it for?*

◆ *People should take a driving test every five years.*

◆ *'Old people shouldn't be allowed to drive – after all, young people aren't allowed to.'*

◆ *If you could own any car you wanted, which would you have? Why?*

Note: *The Driving Instructor* by Bob Newhart is an entertaining introduction to this topic, if you can get a recording of it.

Traditions and festivals

◆ *Every country celebrates Christmas in its own special way. What do you do at Christmas? Do your family all come together? When do you give presents? What do you eat?*

◆ *At what other times of the year do you do something special? Do you dress up in any way? Does your country have a national costume? When do people wear it? Do you have one? What's it like?*

◆ *When was the last time you sent a card? Do you just send them on birthdays?*

◆ *Have you ever been to a wedding? What was it like? How were people dressed? What did they do?*

◆ *What happens on Valentine's Day? Do you send cards?*

◆ *Have you ever received a Valentine card? Was it signed?*

You can also ask your students about any local custom/dress, etc. here.

Money

◆ *Do your parents give you pocket money: if so, how much, or do you have a little job of your own?*

◆ *People are always trying to win money, but what would you do if you won a lot?*

◆ *What would you do if you won a) £10 b) £1,000 c) £20,000 d) £1,000,000?*

◆ *What would your parents do in the same situations?*

◆ *Would winning a lot of money change you as a person?*

Television

◆ *Do you have a television and video at home? How often do you watch every day?*

◆ *Do you know anyone who does not have a television? Why don't they?*

◆ *Describe a typical evening on television in your country? What sort of programmes do you particularly like?*

◆ *Plan an evening's television with all your favourite programmes.*

◆ *If your television was taken away tomorrow what would you do in the evenings instead?*

◆ *'Television has not only destroyed the art of conversation but is also the single biggest factor in teenage violence.' What do you think?*

◆ *Is television basically a good or bad thing?*

◆ *'People are better informed because of TV.'*

◆ *'TV is dangerous – you don't know what is real and what is fantasy.'*

Video

◆ *Do you have a video player? Are you a member of a video club?*

◆ *What was the last programme you recorded on video from TV?*

◆ *How long do you keep programmes you video?*

◆ *What kinds of programmes do you record? Do you swap videos with friends?*

◆ *Are there any videos which you would not watch?*

◆ *Do your parents allow you to record anything you want?*

Travel

◆ *What other countries have you visited? How did you travel? Where did you stay?*

◆ *Have you ever travelled around a country for a month or so? Where did you go? What did you do?*

◆ *Have you ever had a holiday job in another country? What did you do? What was it like?*

◆ *You have won a free ticket for a holiday of your choice. Where would you go?*

◆ *What are the main differences between the people in different countries you have visited?*

Schools

◆ *Have you always been at this school? If not, what were your other schools like?*

◆ *Describe a typical day at school. What do you most like or dislike about school?*

◆ *Make up your ideal weekly timetable.*

◆ *When do children start school in your country? Is this too early/too late?*

◆ *When can you leave school? Do you think this should be changed?*

◆ *What do you most want to see changed in your education system?*

◆ *Is it easy to carry on studying when you leave school? Do you have to pay for further education, or do you get a grant?*

◆ *'Education should be theoretical. Practical education is not real education.' What do you think?*

◆ *'We should learn more/less about other countries/practical things like buying a flat/how to use our free time/other people and how they think…'*

◆ *'It's a waste of time reading Shakespeare/Molière/Goethe nowadays.' Do you agree?*

◆ *Should school be as much like 'the outside world' as possible or not? Why?*

◆ *'Schools encourage competition – that's a bad thing. We should learn to work together in school.'*

Jobs

◆ *Think of as many jobs as you can.*
◆ *Which of these would you think of doing yourself?*
◆ *What's your father's/mother's/brother's/sister's job?*
◆ *Are there any jobs you would not do?*

Note: This topic is very often much less successful than you might expect. Most jobs in fact do not have specific names. The best lessons are those based on a specific activity to do with jobs. There is concrete material for this topic area in Chapter 13 (for example, 'What makes a good job?', balloon debate.)

People: appearance

◆ *Prepare a description of what you look like.*
◆ *Describe the appearance of other people in the class. Describe your teacher.*
◆ *Choose somebody not in your class – a friend or a relative, or a famous person – and describe what they look like.*

People: personality

◆ *Collect adjectives to describe people's characters and talk about some people that you know. What about yourself?*
◆ *What kind of people do you like/dislike?*
◆ *Choose a famous person that the students know and describe his/her personality.*
◆ *Have you ever filled in a personality questionnaire, for example, a computer dating form? What do you think of them?*

Note: There's a computer dating form on page 105.

National characteristics

◆ *Everybody has an idea of a typical French German/Italian/Spanish person. Can you describe all those nationalities? Is what people say about your country true?*
◆ *Are you typical of your nationality? Why/why not? What do people in your country think of people of other nationalities?*
◆ *'Of course you can't generalise about people.' What do you think?*

The cinema

◆ *When was the last time you were at the cinema?What did you see?*
◆ *What kind of films do you like/dislike?*
◆ *How many different kinds of film do you know?*
◆ *If a new film comes out which you want to see, do you go to the cinema to see it or wait until the video is available?*

Music

◆ *What kind of music do you like?*
◆ *Do you play an instrument?*
◆ *What kind of music don't you like?*
◆ *'In a hundred years' time, people will have forgotten all modern pop groups except the Beatles.' Do you agree?*
◆ *Why do people still listen to composers like Mozart, Verdi and Beethoven?*
◆ *'I can't stand pop music – it's just a noise.' Is it?*

Britain

◆ *Have you ever been to Britain?*
◆ *What do you know about London?*
◆ *What is your impression of British people? Do you think they are really like that?*

Note: Remember, the idea of a topic like this is not for the teacher to inform the foreigner about Britain. It is to present some ideas about Britain, or get students talking about Britain in order that they can talk about their own experiences either in Britain or in their own country.

Houses

◆ *Do you have a room of your own?*
◆ *Plan your ideal room.*
◆ *What kind of house/flat do you live in? How many rooms has it got? Describe them. Plan your ideal house. Is it in the town/country? How many rooms has it got?*

Modern inventions

◆ *Make a list of things you use at home which didn't exist a hundred years ago. Which four do you think you could easily do without and which four would you fight to keep?*
◆ *Can you think of anything you would like to see invented? Something to make your life easier which does not exist at present.*
◆ *What about all the people who have been thrown out of work by new inventions – What should we be doing with them?*

Superstitions

◆ *Are you superstitious? Why do you think people are superstitious?*
◆ *Are black cats walking under ladders special for you?*
◆ *Make a list of things that are lucky/unlucky in your country.*
◆ *What about horoscopes? Do you read these/believe in them?*
◆ *Are there any local superstitions/haunted houses/ghosts?*
◆ *Do you believe in UFOs? Have you seen any visitors from outer space or monsters (Loch Ness Monster/Abominable Snowman)?*

The individual

◆ *What is your favourite colour, clothes, music, book, sport, game, film, etc.*
◆ *Pet hates: What really makes you mad? What punishment would you inflict on people who do things that you hate?*
◆ *Do you like/hate to be different from other people?*
◆ *Do you show your individuality?*
◆ *'The worse thing you can say about anybody is that he or she is a conformist.' Do you agree?*

Speech

◆ *Do you have an accent in your own language? What is different about your accent? Do you use any words which are not found throughout the whole country?*
◆ *How many different languages are spoken in your country?*
◆ *'Esperanto – a stupid idea, everyone should learn English.' What do you think?*

Humour

◆ *What sort of jokes do you find most funny/not funny at all?*
◆ *Do you tell jokes about people from other countries?*
◆ *Take along several cartoons: are they funny or not? Why?*

Note: The following topics are most suitable for older classes. Do not attempt them with students younger than sixteen.

Crime

◆ *What would happen to someone in your country who had...*
   (a) stolen a shirt from a local supermarket
   (b) murdered someone
   (c) not paid his or her television licence
   (d) been caught driving while drunk
   (e) broken into a house and stolen jewellery
   (f) hit a child so hard that the child's arm had been broke
◆ *What do you think should happen to people who do those things?*

The environment

◆ *What industries are there near where you live? Is there any pollution from them?*
◆ *Technology: science has moved forward more than ever in the past hundred years and has affected the environment greatly. Make a list of inventions and developments this century. Decide which have been harmful and which have been beneficial.*
◆ *Argue for and against the following:*
   a) no cars in the cities   b) jumbo jets
   c) disposable bottles   d) plastic knives and forks
◆ *Factories that pollute rivers or oil tankers that pollute the sea – which is worst? What should be done about them?*

History

◆ *How long has your country been 'a country'? What is the first important date in its history?*
◆ *Give six important dates in your country's history and say why they're important.*
◆ *Why are these dates important for the world: 570, 1564, 1812, 1789, 1990?*
◆ *Every year, people remember the men and women who died in the two world wars. Do you think they will go on remembering? For how long?*

Politics

◆ *'Politics has no place in school.' Do you agree?*
◆ *What are the main issues in your country's politics at the moment? What are the main political parties in your country? Can you give a short description of their point of view?*
◆ *Have you ever protested against anything or been on a demonstration?*

Military service

◆ *Is there conscription in your country? Who has to do it? For how long? What happens if you refuse to go? Do you know anyone who has refused?*

◆ *'People who refuse to do their military service are traitors to their country.' What do you think?*

◆ *'If you're going to have military service then both men and women should have to do it. Why discriminate against men?' What do you think?*

◆ *If there was another war, would you fight?*

Fame

◆ Take in pictures of famous people: *who are they and why are they famous?*

◆ *Who are the ten most famous people in your country today and why? How many of them will be remembered in a hundred years' time?*

◆ *Name six famous people from history who will always be remembered.*

◆ Play the *Who am I?* game with famous people from the past.

◆ *Is fame the same as success?*

Drinking

◆ *Have you ever drunk any alcohol? What was it and where?*

◆ *Have you parents ever given you any alcohol to drink?*

◆ *'Parents should teach their children how to drink at home.' When is the right time to start to teach children to drink?*

America

◆ *Comparison of English and American words.*

◆ *'America – the only true democracy in western Europe, or the most corrupt country in the world.' What do you think?*

Aid and charity

◆ *Helping developing countries: have you ever given any money to help people in the Third World? Do you know what happens to your money?*

◆ *'The rich countries aren't interested in the poor ones. They buy off their consciences every year with massive amounts of aid but it still isn't enough.' What should the rich countries of the world be doing?*

Progress

◆ *The space race – has it been worth it? What spin-offs have there been?*

◆ *The price of progress – televisions, jumbo jets, big cars, better hospitals, people living longer, plastic everything, washing machines, etc. – Has it all been worth it? What have we lost?*

Advertising

◆ *Have you ever bought something because you saw it advertised?*

◆ *Cigarette and alcohol advertising – do you think it should be banned?*

◆ *Good adverts/bad adverts – have you got a favourite advert? Are there any adverts that you do not like?*

◆ *How do adverts work? Do they affect you?*

Minorities

◆ *Minority groups in your country: are there any and what are they fighting for? Are you a member of any?*

◆ *Immigrants – where do they come from? Why have they come to your country? Do you/they get a fair deal?*

Note: Treat this topic with sensitivity. Remember that some of your class may be immigrants.

Chapter 13 Materials 4: *Photocopiable material*

Notes on activities

Pages 94 to 133 contain 80 photocopiable activities. We begin by giving notes on the different kinds of activities.

Putting in order: activities 1–10
You present a concrete list of items which students have to place in order of importance, value or whatever. These have the advantage of providing the concrete material for the discussions, and by choosing a suitable range of items you can make the discussions wider than would be the case if you relied only on students' personal contributions.

A particular kind of problem which is often very popular and successful is the 'cornflake packet problem'. These are the sort of materials which are often the basis for competitions run by popular magazines or on the back of cereal packets. The basic idea is to 'put the following eight features of an ideal holiday in order of importance. If you think 'sandy beaches' is most important number it 1 …'

Agreeing and disagreeing: activities 11–14
Concrete statements as a basis for discussion.

Group discussions: activities 15–20
These are all suitable for use in a class which has been divided into small groups with a 'secretary' and 'chair' appointed. Discussions may take place in English or their native language, but the reports and subsequent discussion should be in English. You should decide who goes in which group. Decide the distribution of stronger and weaker students to ensure as much activity as you can.

The balloon debate (activity 20) can be played with more advanced classes by putting famous people in the balloon, e.g. Goethe, Marie Curie, Napoleon, Cleopatra, Madonna, Mother Theresa, Newton, Charlie Chaplin.

Questionnaires: activities 21–24
The sort of personality quiz which is common in magazines can be a little childish, too risqué or too difficult linguistically. However, it could provide you with ideas for the kind you can make up yourself. Questionnaires can be presented as reading comprehension or listening comprehension. You should go through them in advance and make up scores of the following type:

30–40 People like you but find you too dominant. You can be fun but people very easily get tired. Anyway, why aren't you a little bit calmer?

87

The explanations should be pitched at the level of the class. The questionnaire itself can be photocopied and distributed or simply read out for students to write down the appropriate answers – *a, b*, etc.

Role-plays: activities 25–27

These are somewhat more difficult and students will require some time to prepare their roles. They will be best used with small groups of older students.

Discussion items: activities 28–31

Short articles or extracts which contain suitable pegs on which to hang a discussion; notice that they are short and suggest an obvious discussion point. Time should not be spent wading through the text in class, it's sufficient for the students to read the text quickly, or even for you to read it aloud for them; it is to form the basis of a discussion, not to swamp the lesson. The examples show you the sort of items which are usually successful.

Pictures: activity 32

The success of pictures depends largely on practical considerations. Make sure your pictures are large enough and you have enough of them. a single picture will usually work in a group of up to eight, but in large groups divide the class and use several pictures. Even in small classes it is advisable to stick pictures on to a piece of firm card. The best pictures can be used for several different purposes with the same or different classes. At lower levels they are used mostly for naming things, describing events or telling a story. At higher levels pictures should be ambiguous, permitting different interpretations to allow the class to speculate or discuss. Colour supplement magazines provide a good source of interesting and varied pictures, but it is important to remember that the main criterion for selection is the language the picture will generate.

Cloze dialogues: activities 33, 34

The students are given a dialogue written out on stencil, overhead transparency or the board, from which certain key words have been deleted. The number and choice of such words depends on the class. Students read the dialogue in pairs adding suitable words to the gaps. In some cases there will only be a single word which will be appropriate in the gap, while in others a choice may be available. Decide in advance if you are going to treat items like *don't* and *she'd* as one or two items. (We prefer to treat them as single items.)

Information-only dialogues: activity 35

Similar to the cloze dialogue, except all non-information words (*please, excuse me, I'm afraid*, etc.) are omitted and only the bare outline of what the speakers mean is left. This is much more difficult than the cloze dialogue, however. You will usually need to discuss it line by line with the class before asking students to read it naturally in pairs. If you write these yourself you should include the minimum information possible and choose situations in which the students may want to use their English themselves.

Situations suitable for information only dialogues include: buying – tickets, something in shops; getting information – at the information bureau, bank, railway station, from a stranger in the street; at home – dialogue at breakfast, over a meal, about a television programme you're watching, when offered something, etc.

Completing the story: activities 36, 37

The teacher tells a story which is contrived so that it describes but does not produce the language needed for various speech events. The students are required to fill in what the characters in the story say at the points where the teacher pauses. In most cases only one phrase is exactly right. After supplying the missing items, students can be encouraged to continue or complete the stories. This type of activity is best done in small groups.

Situations: activities 38, 39

A situation, usually involving two or occasionally three speakers, is described verbally to the students. They must then try to build the whole conversation that would arise out of the circumstances.

Again, however, these situations can vary from the simple: *You want to find out the time of the last train from London to Brighton, but the person you ask is also a stranger*, to a description of a disagreement, argument or formal meeting.

Dialogue writing: activities 40, 41

Give students an outline of a situation. Let them work in pairs or small groups to write a dialogue for the situation. Several pairs perform before commenting, correcting, etc. These activities give a list of situations. Don't do more than one or two at a time.

Who's speaking?: activities 42, 43

A number of similar expressions are listed together with a number of people. Students pair up the expressions and the speakers appropriately. This exercise can be made slightly more difficult by giving only the list of expressions and asking students themselves to provide appropriate speakers.

Possible or impossible?: activity 44

Students in pairs or groups are presented with a series of two-line dialogues. Each question consists of an opening line and four responses. The students mark each of the responses possible or impossible. Possible means this would be a normal, neutral, friendly thing to say to an acquaintance (not a close friend).

The number of possible responses given for the different questions should vary so that none, one, two, three or all four may be correct.

Matching questions and answers: activity 45

Students are presented with questions and answers to match. This activity emphasises the importance of giving a fuller answer that just *yes* or *no*.

Rearranged dialogues: activities 46–51
Particularly for younger students, one of the easiest ways to introduce the idea that a conversation is not just a series of questions and answers is to give them (on an overhead transparency or on the board) the mixed-up lines of a natural dialogue between no more than two people). All students have to do is to rearrange the lines to make a natural dialogue.

The dialogue you use should have most of the lines structurally linked:
A: It's a lovely day, isn't it?
B: Yes, it is, isn't it? But it was very cold yesterday, wasn't it?
A: Yes, it was. I went to London.
B: Oh, did you?

The whole thing can be made much more difficult by including some of the following one word lines:
Really? Please. (on its own) *Sorry?*

Other very short responses (*I'm afraid not. Not really.*) also make it difficult. You could put younger students in teams and see who can rearrange the dialogue most quickly. Although this activity may look rather trivial, you are in fact forcing students to concentrate on the linguistic links which make conversation something more than the information-only type of dialogue. The object of these practices is to make students aware of the fact that what one speaker says is linked to what the previous speaker has said.

Cloze texts: activities 52, 53
We're already discussed cloze dialogues. Here you take a text and delete from it important structural words – auxiliary verbs, irregular past tense forms, etc. and ask students to fill in possible words. Again, you should vary the words you delete. Some should have only one possible answer (*She could have _____ asked*). Others should allow restricted choice (*She _____ have been asked*). Others may have a very wide choice (*She could have been _____*).

If students produce the correct answer, this serves as a useful revision. If they do not, it reveals gaps in their knowledge which you can either deal with yourself or mention to their class teacher. If you make up a text yourself it is possible to have an amusing or exciting story, and by deleting suitable words you can give the students a chance to make the story even more amusing! The easiest way to make these up is to use texts from ordinary textbooks. The most difficult are not usually when you delete difficult words but rather when you delete structural words – *as, though, than* and so on.

Finally, bear in mind that if the text begins, *The _____ curled up on the rug at its master's feet.* There appears to be a free choice between, for example: *dog* and *cat.* If towards the end of the text it *purrs*, all those who have chosen *dog* will have to go back and correct themselves. It can be frustrating but fun for the students to discover that the murder victim was shot after they've given the criminal a knife in the first line!

Spot the difference: activities 54, 55

Students are presented with pairs or small groups of sentences which are similar in meaning. They try to explain the difference. The differences may involve grammar, connotational meaning, register, or on occasions simply be two sentences that look similar but have quite different meanings.

Opposite meanings: activity 56

Very often if we wish to express two opposite meanings, we require two sentences which are quite different in form. Only rarely is one the direct structural negative of the other. Incidentally, this shows very clearly why so many students who are good at English at school still have a lot of trouble speaking fluently and naturally.

Elimination problems: activities 57–59

Students are given a list (an odd number) of words and a series of clues. Each clue takes two words from the list. After solving all the clues the odd word is left. The pairs can be pairs of synonyms, pairs of opposites, two words that make a phrase (*letter box, timetable*) or words that are associated with each other. If you make up such puzzles you should use a preponderance of words which you are sure the students already know. Then add a few that are on the edge of their vocabularies.

Pairing puzzles: activities 60–64

Rather easier than the elimination puzzles are those where students are given two lists, each containing an equal number of items, and have to pair up the corresponding words or expressions. This can be done with synonyms, words of opposite meaning, expressions where one column contains colloquial expressions and the other the 'straight' synonym, or words which are associated.

Colloquial expressions and idioms: activities 65–69

Non-native teachers often think that their students should be taught idioms such as *It's raining cats and dogs*. In fact, they will probably sound very odd if they use expressions like that. Much more useful to the students, more fun to teach, and the sort of thing they like to know, are colloquial expressions – things that native-speakers use naturally in everyday spoken English but which rarely get into textbooks. It's not worth doing whole lessons on these but it is always useful to have two or three up your sleeve for five minutes at the end of a lesson, or if you want a light-hearted break after some more serious activity.

There are basically three ways of teaching idioms:

1 Give the students the expression (write it on the board or say it) and ask, 'What do you think this means?' You will be amused by some of their more comical suggestions, but you can encourage these – they make this a more light-hearted activity.
2 Give them the expression with one or two words missing (like a cloze sentence) and ask them to supply the missing word(s). For example, write on the board *Once in a ——— moon*, then say, 'Here's an expression that

means *very rarely indeed*. What word is missing?'

3   The most comical (and least pedagogically sound!) is to give the expressions in multiple choice form and ask the class to pick the correct expression. This should only be done occasionally and very light-heartedly since, if you're not careful, it will confuse rather than help students. Remember these are for fun with older classes.
Here is a single example:

Jack is a bit dull. He can't do anything without help.
In fact he's rather a:
a) *sick swan*   b) *lame duck*
c) *one-legged gull*   d) *dead hen*

Odd-one-out exercises: activities 70–72
Most of us as children have picked the odd one out from examples like:
apple   pear   banana   potato   peach
This type of puzzle can be exploited in three different ways in the language classroom:
1   For vocabulary when the traditional puzzle items are suitable.
2   Using words which are grammatically similar (see examples in activity 71)
3   To stimulate discussion (in English!). Remember these are language learning activities – not party games – so ambiguity and discussion are positive factors.

Puzzles to stimulate language: activities 73–76
If you decide to use puzzles you should explain to the students that you are concerned with the language they use to solve the puzzle. So, when they get stuck, they must not just sit and look at it or revert to their own language. The objective is that they should discuss, reason and argue in English. Most good bookshops have a selection devoted to puzzled books, often in the children's department. One or two well-chosen books should provide you with a wealth of materials. They are usually particularly easy to find around Christmas time and may well be a source of new ideas for the new term after the Christmas break.

Authentic materials: activities 77, 78
Many activities can be based on brochures, timetables etc, which you have taken with you. The more real these are, the better. Two very basic examples are given to show you only the kind of thing you could do. Other suggestions include:
● Give one student a tourist brochure; others ask when things are open, how much they cost and so on.
● One student has a timetable, the others ask questions.
● A group of students has three or four advertisements for similar things – holidays, places to stay, things to do etc. – and discuss which they prefer.
● Students have information about using the telephone (leaflet or poster) and look for answers to specific questions and/or discuss the best course of action.

Remember that when you use authentic material it may be objected that it can only be used by students whose English is good enough for them to understand it. This is not true. Anyone who wants to understand a train timetable or advertisement needs to do so regardless of the level of their grasp of the language. The important thing is to handle the material in different ways; for less advanced students it's enough if they can get the gist of what they want and the answers to a few specific questions (*Is it open on Sundays? When is the last train?*) Don't forget, these materials will be difficult to get hold of when you are abroad so look for some before you go.

Your philosophy: activities 79, 80

All of us are, if we are honest, egocentric. It is not always easy to talk about ourselves, but with a little prompting most of us can be persuaded to say something, particularly if the questions aren't too serious or threatening. If your students are a little older, we suggest a short personal questionnaire, done individually, then compared in pairs and then reported to the whole class, could provide a good basis for stimulating discussion.

Activity 1

Win £1000 for your holiday

Look at the following list of attractions for your holiday. If you think the most important is 'beautiful scenery', write 1 beside it. Write 2 beside your next choice and so on. Then give one other feature that would specially appeal to you.

Sunshine ☐   English spoken ☐

Beautiful scenery ☐   Interesting history ☐

Sandy beach ☐   Quiet, few people ☐

Amusement arcade/bingo ☐ Good local food ☐

Good discos ☐

Another feature that specially appeals to me is

....

Activity 2

Win £1000

All you have to do is put the nine inventions listed below in the order you think they should go – mark the most useful 1, the next most useful 2 and so on. Then add a new machine which you think would be useful in every home and which no one has invented yet.

Fridge ☐   Electric food mixer ☐

Automatic washing machine ☐ Mobile phone ☐

Freezer ☐   Dishwasher ☐

Vacuum cleaner ☐   Tape recorder ☐

CD player ☐

My new machine is

....

The perfect partner

Everybody has a different idea of the ideal boyfriend or girlfriend.
Put the following qualities in order of importance.

Good looks	☐	Lets you decide things	☐
Patience	☐	Sexiness	☐
Plenty of money	☐	Popular with your family	☐
Interests you both share	☐	Popular with your other friends	☐
A sense of humour	☐		

What makes a good job?

When you're looking for a job, what things will make you think it is the job
for you? Put these in order of importance.

Well paid	☐
Flexible hours	☐
The chance to help other people	☐
Lots of different things to do	☐
Nobody tells you what to do	☐
Long holidays	☐
Lots of friendly people to work with	☐
Power	☐

Activity 5

Help us to help you

We are planning a new magazine for all of you between 13 and 18. We want you to help us to make sure that you really enjoy our new magazine. Look at the features below and decide which is most important for you – number it 1, and so on, down to 9.

A column answering your letters about personal problems ☐

Good sports reports ☐

News about the pop scene ☐

Crosswords and puzzles ☐

Letters from people the same age in other countries ☐

A love story every week ☐

Health and beauty tips ☐

Technical reports about cars and scientific developments ☐

Pull-out posters of your favourite stars ☐

Activity 6

It's a wonderful town

Think about the town you live in. Does it have all the things that you want? What sort of town would you really like to live in? Put the following features of towns in order.

Lots of cinemas ☐

A swimming pool ☐

A good library ☐

Late-night discos ☐

Close to the countryside ☐

Very little traffic ☐

Nice architecture ☐

A good local museum ☐

The ideal school

Look at the following statements about schools. Arrange them in order of importance – so that you will learn a lot and so that you will enjoy school.

School should be about practical not theoretical things. ☐

Television should be used more to make school more interesting. ☐

Teachers should decide what is studied in school, not students. ☐

Everyone should study the same things. ☐

Parents should be allowed to come to classes. ☐

More time should be spent out of school – in the town doing things. ☐

Sport should be given a more important place at school. ☐

Everybody should have to study their own language, mathematics, the history
 of their country and English all the time they're at school. ☐

Schools should organise more social events for students – discos and so on. ☐

If there are any statements that you definitely do not agree with, write a new statement which gives your views about the same subject and put it in your list in the proper place.

Here is the news

Look at the following news items:

Earthquake in Mexico, 200 people killed, 500 homeless

Liverpool wins Football League Championship again

Socialists win French election

Australian Prime Minister kidnapped

Murderer of six people in six months arrested by police at airport

'Sex in cities' – called the most shocking film ever made – to be shown in London cinemas

The Queen's flu is still not better

1 Which order do you think they would come in a British newspaper?
2 Is this the right order?

An important job

Which of the following jobs is the most important in your opinion?
Put them in order:

Doctor	☐	Secretary	☐	Teacher	☐
Police officer	☐	Farm worker	☐	Pop singer	☐
Reporter	☐	Politician	☐	Pilot	☐
Soldier	☐	Dentist	☐	Minister	☐

1 Which of them do you think earns most in your country nowadays?
2 Which of them do you think should earn most? Why?
3 Which of them would you like to do? Which wouldn't you like to do? Why?

A lovely evening

Here are six ways to spend an evening. Mark the one you would most like to do 1, and so on down to 6.

Watching television	☐
Playing tennis	☐
Reading a novel	☐
Having a serious discussion with your family	☐
Working in the garden	☐
Listening to records of Beethoven	☐

Better than all of these would be ....

....

The thing I'd hate to do with an evening is...................................

....

School

Look at the following statements. Mark each one in the following way:
If you agree write 1; if you disagree write 2; if you are not sure about it write 3.

Teachers should keep students quiet in school. ☐

Teachers talk too much. ☐

Wearing uniforms is silly. ☐

If a teacher doesn't know the answer, he or she should say
 'I don't know'. ☐

The best age to start school is seven. ☐

Teachers should teach their subject and not worry about what
 you're wearing, what you're doing and things like that. ☐

Boys and girls should be treated exactly the same at school. ☐

School at the moment is too easy. ☐

School starts too early in the morning. ☐

Men and women

Mark each of these statements: 1 if you agree; 2 if you disagree;
3 if you're not sure.

Men are usually stronger than women. ☐

Women are usually more sympathetic than men. ☐

Women are usually better with children than men. ☐

Women are usually better at running a home. ☐

Men are better at making decisions than women. ☐

Women are more careful than men. ☐

Men lose their temper more easily than women do. ☐

Women waste more time than men do. ☐

Women work harder than men. ☐

Activity 13

Parents and children

Mark each of these statements: ✔ if you agree; ✘ if you disagree; ? if you're not sure.

Most parents ought to be stricter with their children. ❑

Summer holidays without parents are more enjoyable. ❑

Most teenagers are bored with their jobs. ❑

It's best to have a good time before you get married because after that life's pretty dreary. ❑

I learn more from my friends of my own age than I learn from my parents. ❑

Today's teenagers are very different from teenagers in the past. ❑

Teenage boys spend too much time thinking about their clothes and hair. ❑

I'd rather go to my parents for advice than to my friends. ❑

Teenagers should be able to go out in the evening without having to tell their parents where they're going. ❑

Most adults say one thing but do another. ❑

Activity 14

Some students at an international centre in England were asked what they thought about the best and worst characteristics of their own countries. Here are some of their answers – do you agree with them?

'We're a very efficient people, we organise things well. I don't think we have a negative characteristic; people call us nationalistic but I'd say we were just proud of Germany.'
– Helmut, German

'Oh, the Italians are alive. We enjoy life and doing things. In some ways we're a bit too light-hearted, but I think that's a good thing. Live for today – tomorrow's a long way away.'
– Mario, Italian

'We are fair, we always try to see all sides of a problem and to consider everybody. I suppose this makes us a bit slow to offer an opinion sometimes, we're too careful.'
– Torsten, Swedish

'I think we're rather a cruel people – think of bullfighting for example, which I hate. But we're very warm and generous. We try to help people – but we're not very nice to animals.'
– Maria, Spanish

'We have the best food in the world and the most beautiful language in the world. I suppose we've made the biggest contribution to the history of Europe. I can't think of anything negative to say about my country, I think France is marvellous.'
– Nadine, French

Are you a typical member of your own country? Why/why not? What about your father/mother?

Give three adjectives you associate with:
German people   Swedish people
Italian people   Spanish people
French people

Pack a suitcase

Plan what clothes the following people will need to pack:

a) A couple going on their honeymoon in Spain for three weeks in June.
b) A businessman or businesswoman flying to attend a three-day conference in New York in February.
c) A student travelling by train with a rucksack for a month in the summer.
d) An 18-year-old going to stay for a weekend with friends in the country.
e) A young couple going for a ski-ing holiday.

Activity 16

Around the world

Plan a trip around the world. You have as much money as you need! Discuss:

- How will you travel from place to place?
- Where will you go?
- What do you hope to do and see?
- If you could take one (famous) person with you, who would you take? Why?

Activity 17

Cast away

You are going to be cast away on a desert island with a record player and six records (fortunately the island has got electricity!). There will only be three of you on the island, and you have to agree on the six records you are going to take.

Activity 18

Future 2060

It's the year 2060. Everyone has their own personal computer for getting news and information, and your national government has decided that of radio, television and newspapers only one can survive – not just for information but as a form of entertainment. Work in three groups, one each to defend radio, television and newspapers. Work out:

a) Why your medium is important.
b) What sort of service it can give to people which they can't get from their computers.
c) Why your service is better and more useful than the others.

Activity 19

What would your parents do if...?

- You came home at 11 pm.
- You came home at 1 am.
- You smoked in your bedroom.
- You were sent home from school for disturbing the classes.
- You were caught stealing a CD in a local record shop.
- You wanted to have a party with 25 of your friends at home.
- You wanted to get married when you were only 17.
- You wanted to buy a moped.

Activity 20

Balloon debate

A group of people are travelling in a balloon, but it has a small hole in it and is falling. None of the people can swim. They decide one person must be thrown out, so that they can reach the island. Imagine you each have one of these jobs:

politician	hairdresser
vet	chef
ballet dancer	police officer

Prepare a few reasons why you should not be thrown out. How will you help on the island? Why will the group need you? Who will they not need?

After everyone has spoken, vote on who is going to be thrown out.

Activity 21

Are you extrovert?

Answer these questions as honestly as you can. Mark the answer to each of the questions which most closely represents your most usual behaviour or feeling.

a) Very much so   b) Yes   c) Average   d) No   e) Definitely not

1 Do you usually have a quick answer when people talk to you? ❑

2 Are you fond of practical jokes? ❑

3 Do you dislike doing things which have to be done quickly? ❑

4 Are you a lively sort of person? ❑

5 Do you 'look before you leap'? ❑

6 Can you get a party going? ❑

7 Do you like telling funny stories or jokes? ❑

8 Do you dislike spicy foods? ❑

9 Are you rather careless? ❑

10 Do you tend towards pessimism? ❑

11 When someone shouts at you do you shout back? ❑

12 Do you prefer thought to action? ❑

13 Are you rather impulsive? ❑

14 Do you tend to avoid meeting new people? ❑

When you have finished, compare your answers with a partner.

Will you get an invitation?

Everybody likes going to parties, but parties are only successful if the right people are there. Are you one of the right people? Do people want you at their party? Find out by answering these questions. Pick the answer you think is nearest to your view.

1   Who will you spend the evening talking to?
    a) The person who invited you to the party.
    b) As many people as possible.
    c) The girl/boy you went with.
    d) The tall, brown-eyed, dark-haired, really attractive boy/girl you noticed at another party last week.

2   It's a fancy dress party and lots of your school friends will be there. Who will you go as?
    a) Napoleon.
    b) A baby.
    c) Marlene Dietrich.
    d) A Turkish belly dancer.

3   When do you leave the party?
    a) 10 o'clock sharp!
    b) Just after everybody else has gone.
    c) As soon as the beautiful dark-haired girl/boy you were hoping to meet has left.
    d) When you see the sun coming up.

4   At last you've met the girl/boy you were hoping would be at the party. How do you start your conversation?
    a) Where've you been all my life?
    b) Excuse me, do you know where the loo is please?
    c) Do you like dancing?
    d) I collect stamps, what is your hobby?

5   Someone has just picked up their drink. They trip up and it goes all over you. What do you do?
    a) Pour your drink all over them.
    b) Shout at them and call them an idiot.
    c) Say it doesn't matter.
    d) Just give them a dreadful look and don't speak to them for the rest of the evening.

6   Somebody you really don't like comes to talk to you. Do you:
    a) Talk to them politely so you don't upset anybody else.
    b) Say 'Go away, I don't want to talk to you'.
    c) Try to introduce them to someone else.
    d) Go to the loo.

7   You are asked what kind of music you would like to hear:
    a) Something loud and fast that you can dance to.
    b) Something quiet and slow that you can dance to.
    c) Folk songs so that everyone can sing together.
    d) Some Chopin so that you can hear each other speak.

8   While you are dancing to the very fast music, your partner's jeans start to split down the back. What do you do?
    a) Say something immediately and help your partner out of the room.
    b) Wink to the others, but don't tell her/him.
    c) Start laughing out loud and point so that everyone looks.
    d) Ignore it completely and wait for someone else to start laughing.

When you have finished, compare your answers with a partner.

© *Michael Lewis and Jimmie Hill 1993* This page may be photocopied for use in class.

Are you a good citizen?

Life if so much nicer if everyone tries to take a positive part. What about you, do you help other people or not? Here is a questionnaire to help you find out.

1   You see a blind man at the edge of the road. Do you:
   a) Ignore him.
   b) Insist on taking him across the road – even if he says 'It's all right, I can manage thank you'.
   c) Offer to help, but leave him if he says 'I can manage'.
   d) Take him across the road and continue with him to wherever he's going.

2   You see a £10 note lying in the road. Do you:
   a) Pick it up and put it in your pocket.
   b) Take it into the nearest shop and leave it there.
   c) Take it to the police station.
   d) Rush up to the nearest person and ask them if they've dropped it.

3   You see a three-year-old boy crying in the street. Do you:
   a) Walk past.
   b) Phone the police.
   c) Go and try to talk to him.
   d) Go and give him a big cuddle.

4   Your neighbours are moving. Do you:
   a) Take the day off work to help.
   b) Make sure you're out the day that they move.
   c) Leave them to do the job themselves but make them pots of tea.
   d) Get some friends together and all help to carry all the heavy things.

5   You have just started work. Somebody who has worked for the same organisation for 25 years is leaving. Do you:
   a) Organise a collection for a present.
   b) Give a very small donation when somebody asks you to help buy a present.
   c) Say 'But I don't know them'.
   d) Go and explain that you're not giving anything to their present because you don't know them.

6   You see two teenage boys making fun of an old lady on the bus or train. Do you:
   a) Go and tell them to keep quiet.
   b) Look out of the window and pretend nothing's happening.
   c) Try and get an adult to go and do something.
   d) Wait until the boys get off the bus and then go and talk to the old lady.

7   A friend of yours who smokes a lot goes to a party. You know that the people giving the party don't like smoking. Do you:
   a) Tell the friend before she goes that she mustn't smoke.
   b) Stop her when she takes her cigarettes out at the party.
   c) Let her do what she wants – it's nothing to do with you.
   d) Apologise for your friend but don't stop her smoking.

When you have finished, compare your answers with a partner.

Wanted: 1,000 unmarried readers

Free computer test to find your perfect partner

If you're sixteen or over you can take advantage of this unique test, offered to you by Europe's largest computer dating organisation.

Just tell us what you're like and what you want, and our computer will find the perfect partner for you absolutely free!

Within a few days of sending in this free test you will receive the computer's description of your perfect partner.

Your age .... Your sex .... Height .... Colouring ....

Race/Nationality.. Religion..

Occupation ....

First name .... Surname ....

Address ....

Using modern psychology, sociology and computer sciences the computer will compare your personality profile with those of over 60,000 people, detail by detail. Only then will the computer print out a comprehensive and objective description of its choice of the perfect partner for you.

Do you consider yourself (tick ✔ the appropriate boxes):

Shy	☐	Generous	☐	
Extrovert	☐	Outdoor type	☐	
Adventurous	☐	Creative	☐	
Family type	☐	Practical	☐	
Clothes-conscious	☐	Intellectual	☐	

Do you like (tick ✔ the appropriate boxes):

Cinema/theatre	☐	Pop music	☐	
Good food	☐	Sport	☐	
Travel	☐	Do-it-yourself	☐	
Political activities	☐	Camping/hiking/climbing	☐	
Classical music/literature	☐	Voluntary work	☐	

Sandra Collins is 19. She is very keen to become an artist. She applied while she was at school to go to art college, but was turned down. She has been working in a shop for the last six months and finds it very dull. Just after she started at the shop she met Roger. He is a junior sales representative for a nationwide firm. They have been going out regularly for the past six months. Her father does not like Roger. He thinks he is just playing around with his daughter.

Yesterday Roger heard that he had been offered a new job with the firm in the north of England. He has been offered a very large increase of salary to become chief sales representative for a small new area. He is delighted to have such a good opportunity while he is so young (he is 26). He told Sandra and he wants her to go with him – but he is not prepared to get married yet because he thinks Sandra is too young.

This morning Sandra received a letter from an art college saying that they will give her a place from the beginning of the new term. She had almost forgotten this application, but now has a chance to follow her ambition. Unfortunately, the college is in the south-west of England and so she would not be able to see very much of Roger.

Take the part of one of the following people:

Sandra, Roger, Sandra's father, Sandra's mother, Eileen – Sandra's oldest sister.

Sandra's mother got married when she was very young herself and regrets this. She thinks she missed a lot in life because she got married so young.
Eileen is 27 and unmarried and likes Roger very much herself.

Activity 26: Role-play 2

The members of the committee of the local sports centre have just been given £40,000 to spend. They have to decide how to spend the money.

George Andrews

You are a local head teacher. You want the school's football pitches to be improved. You have worked at the same school all your life and are very proud of it. You are also mad about football and thinks everyone else should be too.

Bob Dobbs

You are a boxer. You believe all young boys should learn how to fight. You think all other sports are for girls. Only boxing is a proper 'man's' sport. You argue with everybody.

Ann Brown

You are very annoyed because everyone wants the money to go to boys' sports. You think all young girls should learn to ride. You want to set up a Girls' Riding club. You would use the money to buy two horses and rent stables. You have a horse, and also believe in Women's Lib.

Major Chalmers

You are the chairman of the local Hunting Club. When your members go out hunting foxes they do a lot of damage to farmers' fences. Your club is famous in the area and it needs this money to pay for the damage. They also need new guns.

Mary Black

You don't like Mr Andrews. He will not allow you and the Ladies' Badminton Club to use the school gymnasium to practise. You need the money to buy new equipment and to pay the rent for the hall which the club uses. If you don't get the money the Badminton Club will have to close.

Sam Sned

You are a member of the local golf club. To you, golf is the most civilised of all sports, where you can meet nice people. You think all young boys should be given the chance to play golf as young as possible. You want the money to be spent on setting up a junior golf club for boys between 10 and 16. You do not want girl members.

Rev. Peacock

You run the local Boy Scouts. You try not to disagree with anyone and always try to calm everyone down. But you would like some of the money for your Scouts who want to go to Norway next summer to camp.

Chair, Ms Pamela Gray

You try to encourage everyone to say what they think but you believe the money should be used for quiet, indoor games like chess, darts.

Activity 27 – Role-play 3

You are members of a town-planning committee. You have only £6m to spend on improvements to your town. The committee has to decide at a meeting how the money should be used over the next few years. There are several suggestions, together with their costs which are going to be considered. You only have money for half these suggestions.

1   To build a ring road round the town to take all traffic away from the centre. £2m
2   To build a new town hall in the city centre. £2m
3   To build two large multi-storey car parks near the shopping centre. £.5m
4   To make a large area of the town a pedestrian precinct. £.5m
5   To put bus shelters in the suburbs where people often have to wait a long time for a bus. £.5m
6   To build an indoor swimming pool. £1.5m
7   To employ more staff to keep the town centre tidier. £2m
8   To provide independent shopping advice centre. £1m
9   To build a new youth centre. £1m
10 To build a roller-skating centre. £1m

Arnold Seddon
You are only interested in one thing – sport – and you don't mind what happens providing the swimming pool is part of the scheme which is accepted.

Bernard Bottomly
You are an ex-army officer and you were elected to the committee because you were strongly against private cars. You are used to telling people what to do without discussing. You are very aggressive.

Lilian Chumley
Your special interest is in the housewives and the suburbs. You get very annoyed if people argue for more things for children.

Christine Booth
You are particularly interested in good facilities for children. You want all the improvements to show a real interest in children. You always disagree at meetings with Mrs Chumley.

Sidney Basing-Stoker
You are not interested in how the money is spent, but you like people to discuss things calmly and quietly. You never lose your temper and you try to make everybody else quieter.

Angela Dickens
You think that the town used to be more impressive and important but not enough has been done to make it a nice place to live. You used to live in a bigger and more important town and you want your little town to impress your friends when they visit you.

Act out the meeting. You must put the views given above and you must have the sort of personality suggested for you. After the discussions the committee will vote on how the money is going to be spent.

Activity 28

Read these letters from a teenage magazine. Do you agree with Sylvia's answers?

Dear Sylvia,

Two years ago my grandfather died and my grandmother came to live with us. At first it was fun because she was always giving me small presents, but now she won't leave me alone. She keeps asking about everything I've been doing and always wants me to do jobs for her, running to the shops and so on. I like my gran but she is becoming an awful nuisance. How can I tell her?

'Friendly and 14'

Dear 'Friendly',

You say you are friendly but you don't seem it to me. It sounds to me as if you're being rather mean. When you were getting something out of Gran it was all right, but when she expects something back you don't like it at all. I think perhaps you ought to learn to be a little bit more generous towards other people.

Dear Sylvia,

I am just 15 and have moved into a room of my own at home. The other night I invited some of my friends round to listen to some music, but my father was furious when he found us alone in the room and made us come down to the sitting room. He has told me I am not allowed to have any of my friends in my room without him or my mother being there.

'Embarrassed'

Dear 'Embarrassed',

Your father is obviously worried about you. I am sure he only wants to help. The best thing is to ask one or two of your friends who have rooms of their own what their parents do and then perhaps to ask them if their parents could have a word with your Dad. Try not to get upset. He's only trying to help. It's probably best if you take your friends into the sitting room first and then say, 'Do you mind if we go to my room for a while now?' Then he probably won't worry so much.

Now write your own letter. Give it to your teacher to answer.

Activity 29

The baddies...

- not only smoke but offer cigarettes to other people.
- press drinks or food on someone.
- use lifts and escalators.
- eat a big lunch even when there's a dinner party planned for the evening.
- give sweets to other people's children.
- smoke without permission at table or in other people's cars and houses.
- let smoke drift into someone else's face.
- sympathise or agree with people who say they just can't stop smoking or lose weight.
- don't bother with seat belts on short journeys.

The goodies...

- host parties which offer non-alcoholic drinks and lots of food as well as booze.
- don't smoke.
- provide a substantial salad or other healthy options for slimmers at dinner parties.
- compliment people on losing weight.
- stay away from work and parties if suffering from a bad cold or flu.
- meet friends for lunch at a gym or swimming pool rather than the pub.
- get up early for a jog.
- eat lots of fish and vegetables.
- drink alcohol only at mealtimes.
- walk or cycle rather than using the car.

Who are your goodies and baddies?

Teach drinking at home

Young people should be taught to drink wisely at home, the National Council on alcoholism advises today.

'Young people should neither have their first experience nor acquire their later drinking habits from outside home', says the Council.

'The desire of those parents who wish to bring their children up in an alcohol-free environment must be respected, but teetotal parents must recognise that in our present culture and environment their children will be confronted with alcohol and a personal decision about its use,' continues the report.

It certainly cannot be taken for granted that children will accept their parents' views,' the report says. 'In fact it is more likely that they will react against them.'

Life 'Too Quiet' for Millionaire

The former footballer who built up a 49-store supermarket chain before selling it for £3,750,000 has been driven back into business after just eight months by boredom, according to his son, Kevin, 25.

Asked why, he said 'I've never done nothing, and I'm not starting now.'

Do you like doing nothing?

Is it better to be strict and stop your children doing things like that, or to encourage them to try while you're there to keep an eye on them?

Activity 31

Newspaper headlines have a peculiar style of their own. So much is omitted that you can be in considerable doubt as to what you are going to read.
What do you think these articles are about? Can you say the headlines in simpler English?

Airgun ban urged

Pay row hits press

Door slammed on talks

Pay deal shelved

Egg talks broken off

Murderer given life

Axed boss hits back

Water board under fire

Flu sweeps London

PM stuck in jam

a) What are these people doing?

b) A crime was committed in the street at ten o'clock yesterday. What were they doing when it happened?

c) The bank was robbed at ten o'clock. A policeman has come to investigate. (One student interviews others in groups). What did the policeman tell his wife that night when he went home and she asked 'Did anything exciting happen today?' Work in pairs and continue the conversation.

Activity 33

An invitation

A: _____ going out this evening?

B: That'd be _____.

A: Is there anywhere you'd _____?

B: No, I'll _____ it to you.

A: _____?

B: Well I think I'd _____go for _____to eat, if _____.

A: Fine. That _____ me.

Activity 34

A: What time _____ it, Jill?

B: _____ about ten to.

A: ___ __ _____?

B: No, ten to twelve.

A: _____, is it as late as that? We really _____ be going.

C: _____ ? Would _____ a cup of _____ before you _____?

A: _____. The last bus goes _____ a few minutes. I think we'd _____ go _____.

C: Well, it's been _____ seeing you again. I hope we _____ meet again _____.

A: Yes, that _____ nice, but you _____ come _____ to us next time.

C: Oh thanks _____'d be _____.

A: _____ we'll _____ be _____. Thanks again.

© *Michael Lewis and Jimmie Hill 1993* This page may be photocopied for use in class.

Activity 35

Charles wants a newspaper. He's in the newsagent's.

CHARLES: *The Daily Telegraph.*
WOMAN: There aren't any left.
CHARLES: What else have you got?
WOMAN: *The Times* and *The Mirror.*
CHARLES: *The Times.*
WOMAN: Twenty pence.
CHARLES: (Gives her a £5 note) I've no change.
WOMAN: I can't change that.
CHARLES: Oh, where can I get it changed?
WOMAN: I don't know.
CUSTOMER: There's a bank on the corner.
CHARLES: Oh! (He turns to leave and bumps into a woman
          with a baby. He goes out.)

Sue is at the railway station.

MAN: Yes?
SUE: I want to go to London.
MAN: What sort of ticket do you want?
SUE: A return.
MAN: Are you going now?
SUE: Yes.
MAN: Are you coming back today?
SUE: Yes.
MAN: Four pounds fifty.
SUE: When is the next train?
MAN: I don't know. Ask at the information office.

Activity 36

Mrs Rogers was rather old. She found it difficult to hurry and when she got to the station it was late. She wasn't sure where to get the train so she asked (1) _____. The man told her it was platform seven. She was struggling with her bag when a young man said, (2) _____. She thanked him and he took her case and put it on the train for her. The train was very crowded. The young man saw two empty seats so asked a man sitting nearby (3) _____. The man said 'No', so the young man took one seat and Mrs Rogers the other. She thanked the young man. (4) _____ he answered. It was very warm on the train and the man sitting beside Mrs Rogers asked (5) _____. Mrs Rogers said 'No' so he opened the window. The young man took out his cigarettes but the other man said (6) _____. The young man, who hadn't noticed, said (7) _____ and put the cigarettes in his pocket again. Then he decided to go for a cup of coffee. He offered to bring Mrs Rogers one but she wasn't thirsty so she said (8) _____. It was so crowded the young man though he might lose his seat while he was away so he asked Mrs Rogers (9) _____. (10) _____ she said, and the young man went to the buffet car. Mrs Rogers was nervous. She didn't often travel on trains. She asked the man (11) _____. He told her he thought it was about two hours. Then he took a timetable out of his pocket (12) _____ he said. 'Oh, thank you very much,' Mrs Rogers said. Suddenly the train stropped. The man looked out of the window. (13) _____ asked Mrs Rogers. 'There's something on the line,' the man told her. I can't see what it is but it looks like (14) _____.

Activity 37

It was dark and it was late. Jack was standing at the bus stop. A man came up to him. He had an unlit cigarette in his mouth. (1) _____ he asked, rather aggressively. Jack felt in his pockets but he had no matches (2) _____ he said. (3) _____ asked the man even more aggressively. Jack, who didn't know that part of the town at all well, said (4) _____. He tried to be pleasant but the man seemed very odd. (5) _____ he asked. 'About five to twelve,' Jack told him. 'There's a bus in a few minutes.' 'Is there? Well you're not going on the bus. You're coming with me, said the man. (6) _____ asked Jack. 'I said you're coming with me,' said the man, taking hold of Jack's arm. (7) _____ shouted Jack angrily. (8) _____ 'And I'll hurt you more if you don't keep quiet,' the man said. Suddenly a car swung into the road. It was driving very fast. It stopped just beside Jack and the man. Someone wound the window down. (9) _____ the driver said. (10) _____ shouted Jack. But, although he struggled furiously the man pushed him into the car.

Activity 38

What would you say in each of these situations? In most cases there is a particular phrase which is always used. Remember particularly that if you translate what you say in your own language it may sound very odd:

1 Someone says to you, 'This is Jill.' You've never met her before. What do you say?
2 A friend says, 'You haven't met my grandmother before, have you?' You haven't. What do you say?
3 Mr Brown says, 'How do you do' to you. What do you answer?
4 What do you say when someone says, 'Hello, how are you?'
5 You're meeting a friend. You're a quarter of an hour late. What do you say?
6 You're sitting on a bus, next to the window. Someone is sitting next to you. You want to get off. What do you say?
7 You help someone to carry a heavy bag. He says, 'Thank you very much'. How do you answer?
8 You don't hear what someone says. You want her to say it again. What do you say?
9 You answer the telephone and give your number. The other person says, 'I'm so sorry, I've got the wrong number'. How do you answer?
10 You're meeting a friend. She arrives late and says, 'I'm so sorry I'm late, I missed the bus'. What do you say?
11 Somebody asks you the time. You haven't got your watch on. What do you say?
12 It's a friend's birthday. What do you say?

Activity 39

What would you say in each of these situations? In most cases there is a particular phrase which is always used. Remember particularly that if you translate what you say into your own language, it may sound very odd:

1 It's the third of January. You meet someone you haven't seen since Christmas. What do you say to them?
2 How do they answer?
3 A friend has just taken the driving test and passed. What do you say?
4 Your friend failed the test. What do you say this time?
5 You're with a friend at home, who says, 'Can you pass me the whatsit please?' You don't know what she wants. What do you say?
6 You've been visiting a friend for the evening. It's getting late and you think you should be going soon. You want to warn the friend. What do you say?
7 A friend asks to borrow your pen. What do you say as you pass it?
8 You pour a cup of coffee for a friend. What do you say when you pass that? (Remember this time your friend hasn't asked for it.)
9 You asked a friend to post a letter for you yesterday. You want to check if he really did post it.
10 He forgot it! What does he say?
11 You have accepted his apology. What do you say.
12 Somebody says 'You're Jack/Janet Waters aren't you?' You aren't! What do you say?

Activity 40

1 *A* and *B* are discussing how to spend the evening. *A* suggests they should both go to the cinema. *B* wants to save money for his/her holidays and suggests they stay at home and listen to some records. *A* agrees.

2 *A* and *B* have just been to the cinema. *A* is very enthusiastic about the film and especially about the star. *B* thinks the film was too long and wasn't impressed by the star. They disagree – but in a very pleasant way. *A* starts: 'What did you think of that then?'

3 *A* and *B* are friends. They sometimes play tennis together.

A: You are going away with your parents on Friday afternoon this week and won't be back until late on Sunday evening. You're free next weekend, except on Friday when you've promised to visit your grandmother.

B: You ask *A* to play tennis with you this weekend. You're free all weekend, but Saturday afternoon would suit you best. You can't play next Saturday because you're taking part in a swimming competition, but you are free next Friday and Sunday.

4 *A:* You've been standing in a shop waiting to be served for five minutes. *B* comes in and pushes past you and begins to talk to the assistant. Start, 'Excuse me, I think I'm first', then continue.

B: *A* has been standing in a shop waiting. You are in a terrible hurry to catch a train. You rush in and start to talk to the assistant. *A* speaks to you but you are in a very bad mood and you just ignore him/her, at least the first time he/she speaks.

5 *A* and *B*, who do not know each other, are sharing a table in a pizzeria.

A: You want a cigarette before your meal but you have no matches with you. You ask *B*.

B: You are in the middle of your lunch. You don't smoke and you don't like people who smoke in restaurants – what's more, you always tell them what you think.

6 *A* and *B* who do not know each other are on a train. *A* wants to do certain things. *B* agrees or disagrees politely:
a) *A* wants to open the window (*B* agrees).
b) *A* wants to smoke, although it's a non-smoking compartment (*B* disagrees).
c) *A* wants to borrow *B*'s newspaper (*B* agrees).
d) *A* wants to move *B*'s case to make more room (*B* agrees).

7 *A* and *B* are two students who are travelling around Europe by train. They do not know each other but have been travelling together for three days. They're in Vienna. *A* has already been to Italy and Greece. *B* has been in Germany and up to Copenhagen. They both have two more weeks' travelling left. They are trying to decide where to go next and whether to go together or to separate. *A* starts, 'I think I might go through Nice and Monte Carlo to Marseilles and then on to Spain'.

8 *A* and *B* bump into each other in a department store. They apologise, then they look at each other. Each is sure that she/he has seen the other person before but can't remember where or when. *A* says, 'Excuse me, haven't we met before?' In fact, they met two years before on a summer holiday/course.

Activity 41

1 You are in a train compartment with an elderly woman, a young girl and a tough-looking man of about 20. He starts to smoke although it is a non-smoking compartment. The elderly lady asks him to stop but he refuses rudely. Help her.

2 You are travelling by train. You have bought a return ticket (cost £6.50) but when the inspector comes to check it you cannot find it. Try and convince the inspector you are not cheating.

3 You have just finished a meal in a pizzeria. Neither the service nor the food has been very good. When the waiter brings the bill you find there is a mistake in it. Complain and ask for a new bill.

4 There are two of you. An English-speaking friend (American or English) has asked your advice – what are the possibilities in your country for him to get a job. Advise your friend.

5 A friend invited you to a party last Saturday but you couldn't go. You were in a hurry when she asked you and didn't have time to explain why not. The reason was because you already had an invitation to someone else you both know very well, but this other person didn't invite the first friend to her party. Now she has heard about it and is rather upset. She thinks you tried to avoid visiting her and kept the other invitation secret. Another friend has told you she's very upset.
Take the parts of the two friends. One telephones the other to clear the air.

6 A couple of teenagers in leather jackets and dirty jeans come up to you at a railway station and asks if they could 'borrow' £2 for their fare home. You do not believe they intend to return it to you and you refuse politely but firmly.

Who's speaking?

Look at the expressions in column A.
Can you pair them up with the speakers in column B?

A

1 What's your name?
   What name is it please?
   I'm afraid I didn't catch your name.
   Who's calling please?
   I'm afraid I don't know your name.

2 It's a great pleasure to meet you.
   Hi there.
   How do you do.
   Hello.
   Good morning.

3 Close the door, would you?
   Would you mind closing the door please?
   Would you close the door please?
   Can you close the door, please?

4 Sorry, there's no smoking in here.
   Excuse me, I'm afraid smoking isn't allowed in here.
   Haven't you seen the sign?
   Oh, you're not going to smoke, are you?

5 Give us a hand.
   Do you mind giving me a hand with this, please?
   Could you please help me?
   Would you help me with this, please?

B

1 A person speaking on the phone
   A hotel receptionist
   A person at a party
   A teacher
   Someone who has already told you
      his/her name

2 Your brother
   Your bank manager
   Someone you are introduced to
   A visitor in your office
   A very important person

3 A stranger
   A colleague
   A good friend
   Your wife or husband.

4 A very good friend
   A rude stranger
   A polite stranger
   The ticket collector

5 Someone you're annoyed with
   A colleague
   A good friend
   A stranger

Who said it?

When do we say the following expressions?

1. a) Can I open the window please?
   b) Could I open the window please?
   c) Would you mind if I opened the window please?
   d) I think I'll open the window if you don't mind.
   e) Goodness, it's so hot in here isn't it.

2. a) Bottoms up!
   b) Your very good health.
   c) Cheers.
   d) Round the teeth, round the gums, look out stomach here it comes.

3. a) I'm not sure I follow you.
   b) What the hell do you mean by that?
   c) Sorry, I'm not with you.
   d) I'm afraid I don't understand.
   e) I'm afraid I don't see what you're getting at.

4. a) You're wrong.
   b) Are you quite sure?
   c) I think you're mistaken there, actually.
   d) That just isn't true.

5. a) Do you think you could possibly move your bag please?
   b) Would you mind moving your bag?
   c) Would you mind moving your bag, please?
   d) Oh come on now, get your bag out of the way.

6. a) I'm so sorry to hear that.
   b) What a pity.
   c) Tough luck!
   d) Hard cheese!

7. a) No.
   b) No, I haven't.
   c) No, I'm afraid I haven't.
   d) No, I most certainly have not.

Activity 44

Look at these two-line dialogues. In each case mark each reply *P* if you think it is a possible reply. If you think it is impossible mark it *I*. There may be one, two, three or four possible answers, or they may all be impossible. A possible answer is something you could say to a stranger or an acquaintance.

1 A: Hello John, how are you?
   B: a) Thank you, very well.
      b) Fine thanks and you?
      c) Very fine thanks. And you?
      d) Not very well.

2 A: Excuse me, do you mind if I open the window?
   B: a) No, please do.
      b) No, that's all right.
      c) Yes, please.
      d) No, I don't mind.

3 A: Caroline sends her regards.
   B: a) Oh.
      b) Send them back.
      c) If you see her give her my regards.
      d) Thank you very much.

4 A: Do you mind if I open this window?
   B: a) No.
      b) I'd rather you didn't.
      c) Please don't.
      d) I don't want you to, please.

5 A: Excuse me, could you tell me the time please?
   B: a) No, I can't.
      b) No, it isn't possible.
      c) I'm sorry I'm afraid I can't.
      d) I'm afraid I haven't got my watch on.

6 A: I'm so sorry I'm late.
   B: a) Oh, that's quite all right.
      b) It doesn't matter.
      c) I see.
      d) Oh, don't worry. It's all right.

7 A: Please have some more.
   B: a) No.
      b) No, thank you.
      c) I'm sorry but I just couldn't manage any more.
      d) No thank you. I've had enough of it.

8 A: Would you mind opening the window please?
   B: a) Certainly.
      b) Yes.
      c) It's my pleasure.
      d) Not at all.

9 A: I'm just back from Italy.
   B: a) I see.
      b) Are you?
      c) How interesting.
      d) Italy?

10 *On the phone*
   A: Hello, could I speak to Jane please?
   B: a) This is her.
      b) It's me.
      c) You're speaking to her.
      d) Speaking.

11 *In the café*
   A: Yes?
   B: a) Could I have a cup of tea please?
      b) Please could I have a cup of tea?
      c) Could I please have a cup of tea?
      d) Tea please.

12 *On a train*
   A: Terrible day, isn't it?
   B: a) Yes, awful, isn't it.
      b) Do you really think so?
      c) Yes, it is.
      d) It is, isn't it.

13 A: Have you heard, I've failed my driving test again.
   B: a) I'm sorry.
      b) Oh, I am sorry.
      c) That's a pity.
      d) Please accept my condolences.

14 A: I thought you'd like a ticket, so I got one for you.
   B: a) Thank you.
      b) That's good.
      c) Oh, thank you very much, that was kind of you.
      d) I'm pleased because I hadn't seen it.

Activity 45

Remember how important it is not to answer just *Yes* or *No* on its own.
A normal friendly reply is much longer. Match the answers in column A with
the questions in column B.

A

1 Was it late?
2 Did they get there on time?
3 Was he angry?
4 Did he appreciate it?
5 Did she like it?
6 Is it on tonight?
7 Are they disappointed?
8 Do you have to wear a tie?
9 Does it cost a lot?
10 Does she work here?

B

a) Yes, it does as a matter of fact.
b) Yes, he was as a matter of fact.
c) Yes, she does, only part time, though.
d) Yes, it was actually.
e) Yes, you do I'm afraid.
f) Yes, she did actually.
g) Yes, they did actually.
h) Yes, they are a bit.
i) Yes, it is as a matter of fact.
j) Yes, he did as a matter of fact.

Activity 46

Rearrange these lines to make a natural dialogue.
Write the correct order in the box.

1 Did you. How's she?
2 Didn't you?
3 Yes, it is, isn't it. I've just been shopping.
4 Hello, it's a lovely day, isn't it.
5 Did she! No, I didn't know.
6 Have you. Did you buy much?
7 Oh, very well. You know she had a baby last month.
8 No, not much really. But I met Paula.

Now read the dialogue aloud.

Activity 47

Rearrange these lines to make a natural dialogue.
Write the correct order in the box.

1 Oh, I don't really know. Are you going out?
2 Are you? I didn't know you two knew each other.
3 What are you doing this evening?
4 Yes, I am actually. I'm going out with Mary.
5 Didn't you. Oh, yes, we've been seeing a lot of each other recently.
6 Have you! Did you meet at work?
7 Was it really! He didn't tell me he had a party.
8 No we didn't as a matter of fact. It was at John's.

Now read the dialogue aloud.

Activity 48

Rearrange these lines to make a natural dialogue. Write the correct order in the box.

1 Can you! That's interesting.
2 Wouldn't you? I'd go again.
3 Yes, you are, aren't you … unfortunately.
4 I've just been to Majorca.
5 No, you wouldn't, would you. I can understand that.
6 Have you. I'd never go there.
7 Yes it is, isn't it. I'm beginning to understand you.
8 Would you? I wouldn't go once, never mind twice!

Now read the dialogue aloud.

Activity 50

Rearrange these lines to make a natural dialogue. Write the correct order in the box.

1 You sound surprised.
2 As well as can be expected, thanks.
3 Shocking day isn't it?
4 Are you really?
5 Really. And you had bad weather there.
6 Italy.
7 Not too bad thanks. Are you keeping well?
8 We did.
9 I am a bit. I thought you liked comfort.
10 Did you? How disappointing. Where did you go?
11 We are going camping this year.
12 We do. Don't worry, it's a very modern caravan.
13 Isn't it awful, we've just come back from our holiday and we had awful weather all the time.
14 Hello, how are you?

Now read the dialogue aloud.

Activity 49

Rearrange these lines to make a natural dialogue. Write the correct order in the box.

1 That's right, the one when Bob got married.
2 Really? It's not often that happens, is it.
3 I can't remember what, but I do remember when.
4 Yes, I remember that.
5 Oh yes, it was at that party.
6 John and I couldn't agree, I'm afraid.
7 No, the last time was about two years ago.
8 Do you? What was it about?

Now read the dialogue aloud.

Activity 51

Rearrange these lines to make a natural dialogue. Write the correct order in the box. The first and last lines of this dialogue are in the correct place.

1 Hello.
2 Yes, I'm afraid so.
3 Not bad thanks. Chilly this morning, isn't it?
4 Oh, much better thanks.
5 Oh, don't worry. It could have been worse.
6 Awful, isn't it? John was telling me the other day you'd hurt yourself.
7 Well, I've been a bit off colour myself recently.
8 What on earth did you do?
9 Really? What a dreadful nuisance.
10 Fine, thanks – and you?
11 Really? Nothing serious I hope.
12 How are you feeling now?
13 Oh, it wasn't serious, I just twisted my ankle.
14 Hello, how are you?
15 Oh no – it's this bug that's been about, you know. I feel better now. I think I'll survive.

Now read the dialogue aloud.

Activity 52

Fill in one word in each space in the following. Sometimes there is only one correct word but sometimes you have a choice of words.

The Future

By the end of the twenty-first _____ there _____ well be people living in _____ who _____ never visited Earth, but _____ that they can _____ in touch with _____ families, _____ they happen to be _____ Earth, the moon, or _____ else in the system, because _____ will all _____ wearing a wristband. Through this, _____ a _____ orbiting computer, _____ will be able to talk to any _____ person in the solar system, _____ by speaking that person's computer number _____ their wristband. Their wristbands can be _____ _____ the million at a cost of only about £15 each. It is difficult to _____ that it is _____ more _____ twenty years _____ the first satellite was _____.

Activity 53

Fill in one word in each space. Sometimes there is only one correct answer, but sometimes you have a choice of words.

The haunted house

_____ house is haunted. It _____ been for _____ two years now. Well _____, the house isn't haunted but the garage _____. I'm not _____ about it, _____ I know the ghost is friendly. I _____ hear him laughing, that's the _____ annoying thing, because he has a very _____ laugh and you _____ hear it all _____ the house. I've _____ seen him but I'd like to. I don't know _____ who has met _____. All _____ friends think it would be _____ to meet this _____ . The first time I _____ he was _____ was two years _____. _____ the middle _____ the night, with no warning at all, I _____ this loud laugh.

© *Michael Lewis and Jimmie Hill 1993* This page may be photocopied for use in class.

Activity 54

Explain the difference between the following pairs or groups of sentences.

1 The car stopped when the lights changed.
   The car was stopping when the lights changed.

2 They live in Dortmund.
   They're living in Dortmund.

3 I've already waited for half an hour.
   I've already been waiting for half an hour.

4 I watched the television until 10 o'clock.
   I was watching the television until 10 o'clock.

5 He lived in Florence.
   He used to live in Florence.

6 I'm leaving tomorrow.
   I'll leave tomorrow.
   I'm going to leave tomorrow.
   I leave tomorrow.
   I'll be leaving tomorrow.

7 I'll be annoyed if he doesn't come.
   I'd be annoyed if he didn't come.

8 I used to live in that part of the town.
   I'm used to living in that part of the town.

9 I didn't see her, did you?
   I haven't seen her, have you?

10 I like to go to the theatre.
   I'd like to go to the theatre.

Activity 55

Explain the difference between the following pairs or groups of sentences.

1 I have lunch at work.
   I'm having lunch at work.

2 I always meet her at the station.
   I'm always meeting her at the station

3 You mustn't do that.
   You needn't do that.

4 Would you like a cake?
   Would you like some cake?

5 Someone in the office will be able to help you.
   Anyone in the office will be able to help you.

6 There are too many shadows in this photograph.
   There's too much shadow in this photograph.

7 What are you doing?
   What do you do?

8 Is there time to catch the train?
   Is it time to catch the train?

9 He stopped to smoke.
   He stopped smoking.

10 She's worked hard recently.
   She's hardly worked recently.

Making opposites

Sometimes making opposites is easy:
I can swim. I can't swim.
But sometimes the opposite is quite different:
Would you like some more tea?
Yes please. No, thank you.

Say what B should say to give the opposite meaning in these cases:

1 A: Would you like to come to a party on Saturday?
  B: Oh, yes thank you, I'd love to.

2 A: Excuse me, do you know where the station is, please?
  B: Certainly, it's just down there on the right.

3 A: Do you mind if I open the window?
  B: No, not at all, please do.

4 A: You don't mind if I bring a couple of friends with me, do you?
  B: No, of course not, that'd be really nice.

5 A: You've met John before, haven't you?
  B: Yes, we've met. Hello again.

6 A: Could you change a pound, please?
  B: With pleasure, just a moment please.

7 A: You can speak French, can't you?
  B: Yes, I learned at school.

8 A: What time do you make it please?
  B: It's about twenty-past three.

9 A: You've got the tickets, haven't you?
  B: Yes, they're in my pocket.

10 A: I suppose you'll be there on Saturday.
  B: Yes, of course.

Cross out two words in the box for each clue. Which word are you left with when you have crossed out the ten pairs?

Clues
a) two animals
b) two colours
c) two fruits
d) two people
e) two things to travel on
f) two things to read
g) two meals
h) two things to wear
i) two pieces of furniture
j) two things you will find on the table at dinner time

dog	green	supper
boat	horse	orange
blue	woman	jacket
child	spoon	trousers
lamp	chair	breakfast
knife	apple	telephone
plane	letter	magazine

Activity 58

Cross out two words from the list for each clue. Which word are you left with when you have crossed out the ten pairs?

Clues
a) Two musical players
b) A book of numbers
c) You use it to check when the train leaves
d) You send a lot when you're on holiday
e) The answers to d) arrive through this
f) Two words, one British one American, for the same thing
g) Two words, one modern one old-fashioned, for the same thing
h) You might see it on a chimney
i) You must have one before you use a car
j) Two opposites

box	letter	bottle
lift	aerial	wireless
post	record	television
time	driving	cassette
cards	boring	directory
radio	elevator	interesting
table	licence	telephone

Activity 59

Cross out two words from the list for each clue. Which word are you left with when you have crossed out the ten pairs?

Clues
a) Two opposites
b) They mean the same
c) They rhyme
d) An American looks for post here
e) They sound the same
f) Two fish
g) There is a silent letter in each
h) Two animals
i) They begin with the same letter
j) Two trees

fir	sole	foreign
fur	soul	salmon
box	near	whale
cow	bear	plaice
now	mean	sound
male	lamb	reliable
mail	beech	generous

Warning! You may have to think twice about some of these clues.

Activity 60

Make pairs of opposites using one word from list A and one word from list B.

A	B
heavy	polite
easy	plump
special	bent
straight	difficult
enormous	dull
slim	light
funny	ugly
sharp	ordinary
gorgeous	tiny
rude	blunt

Activity 61

Make pairs of opposites, using one word from list A and one word from list B.

A	B
tall	slow
fat	interesting
fast	open
dark	light
dull	thin
closed	narrow
easy	unpleasant
nice	difficult
weak	short
broad	strong

Activity 62

Look at the following list of words. There are 13 pairs of opposites and one-odd-one out. Can you give the opposite of the odd word?

poor	serious	cowardly
slim	plump	doubtful
cruel	minute	silent
rigid	enormous	wealthy
noisy	flexible	disastrous
certain	sensible	courageous
scarce	ignorant	successful
coarse	abundant	well-informed
smooth	humorous	pig-headed

Activity 63

Cross out 13 pairs of opposites from the following list of words, then give the opposite of the odd one out yourself.

loud	urban	complex
rude	direct	ordinary
slim	polite	cramped
matt	simple	doubtful
quiet	lenient	aggressive
rural	precise	spacious
stout	certain	approximate
strict	unusual	conventional
shiny	radical	roundabout

Activity 64

Look at the expressions in column A. Can you make correct pairs with the explanations in column B? All the expressions are to do with the weather.

A	B
It's drizzling	It's very hot
It's rather muggy	It's very cloudy
It's clouding over	It's a bit foggy
It's sweltering	It's raining – but only a little
It's pouring	It's raining a lot
It's misty	It's hot and sticky
It's overcast	The weather's getting better
It's clearing up	The weather's getting worse

Activity 65

Where would you be?

Where would you be if somebody said the following to you:

1 'Last orders please.'
2 'All change! All change!'
3 'How would you like the money?'
4 'Rare, medium, or well-done?'
5 'Could I see your boarding card please?'
6 'Would you take a seat for a moment, please?'
7 'Going down?'
8 'Hold tight.'
9 'Do you want mash with it?'
10 'Trying to connect you.'
11 'Do you want to register it?'
12 'Would you like to try it on?'
13 'I'm afraid we're out of stock at the moment.'
14 'Dressing?'
15 'How would you like it done?'
16 'Have you got the odd three please?'

Activity 66

How would you answer?

What would you say to someone who said one of the following to you:

1 'Does that ring a bell?'
2 'What's the catch?'
3 'Do you get the point?'
4 'I hope I'm not butting in.'
5 'Do you mind if we put it up a bit?'
6 'Nippy, isn't it.'
7 'Can I square-up with you later?'
8 'I'm a bit peckish, aren't you?'
9 'Can I top you up?'
10 'What's the damage?'

Activity 67

A funny sort of person...

What do these expressions tell you about someone? Perhaps what kind of person he or she is, what he or she has just done, the clothes he or she is wearing, or whatever.

S/he's...

1 on the fiddle
2 on the dole
3 in a huff
4 round the bend
5 in the soup
6 off his/her rocker
7 a bit uptight
8 up to his/her eyes
9 scruffy
10 on his/her last legs
11 really on the ball
12 a bit sheepish
13 a bit browned off
14 completely stumped
15 a bit thin on top
16 a bit long in the tooth
17 in a rut
18 over the moon

Activity 68

How would I feel if I said:

1 'I feel a bit off colour.'
2 'I've got pins and needles.'
3 'I was absolutely fuming.'
4 'I was really fed-up by the time we'd finished dinner.'
5 'I've just have my jacket pinched.'
6 'I haven't got a leg to stand on.'
7 'I feel lousy.'
8 'He told me to pull my socks up.'
9 'I had to put my foot down.'

Activity 69

What makes you say that?

Can you say something – either a single thing or perhaps a short conversation – that would make me say...

1 'Come off it.'
2 'No thanks, I'm just looking.'
3 'Not up to now.'
4 'I'm afraid it's not up to me.'
5 'OK please yourself.'
6 'I'm not sure, but he must be getting on a bit.'
7 'I'm sorry, I'm broke.'
8 'Oh nothing much, how about you.'
9 'I'm sorry, I just couldn't make it.'
10 'I'm picking up now thank you.'
11 'OK, let's put it off then.'
12 'I don't see how I can get out of it.'
13 'I'm afraid it was a total write-off.'
14 'Well, you'd better keep your fingers crossed then.'
15 'Come on, that was below the belt.'
16 'I don't think I could face it.'
17 'I'll give you a buzz then.'
18 'Touch wood.'

Activity 70

Find the odd word out in each of the following. You need to think about the meaning of each word.

1 car, lorry, train, caravan, van.
2 massive, enormous, minute, huge, gigantic.
3 record, coin, stamp, wheel, ring.
4 veal, lamb, ham, pork, beef.
5 bough, bush, leaf, twig, trunk.
6 bag, case, wallet, briefcase, rucksack.
7 train, plane, car, taxi, bus.
8 blink, yawn, wink, squint, stare.
9 checked, striped, woollen, spotted, plaid.
10 spanner, saw, screwdriver, pliers, nails.
11 generous, honest, deceitful, kind, sympathetic.
12 rush, hurry, gallop, stagger, dash.
13 shriek, clatter, gabble, mumble, yell.
14 mare, cow, sow, ewe, dog.

Activity 71

Find the odd word out in each of the following. You will need to think about the grammar of each word.

1 got, were, had, are, can.
2 attractive, light, green, old, black.
3 quick, sharp, careful, hard, beautiful.
4 sheep, child, horse, woman, man.
5 hit, cut, put, let, sit.
6 cost, read, shut, hurt, tell.
7 alike, attentive, aloud, asleep, awake.
8 snow, advice, weather, furniture, apple.
9 yours, ours, theirs, hers, my.
10 walk, write, visit, cook, push.
11 boy, book, house, child, dog.
12 content, satisfied, associated, pleased, natural.
13 socks, trousers, scissors, shirts, gloves.
14 proper, perfect, polite, popular, personal.
15 news, women, people, sheep, cattle.
16 important, impartial, impertinent, impolite, imperfect.

Answers: *cut this off before you give it to the class.*

1 *got* – the others are auxiliaries.
2 *attractive* – it's not -er comparative.
3 *hard* – the others make adverbs with -ly.
4 *horse* – it's the only regular plural.
5 *sit* – the others have principal parts the same.
6 *tell* – the others have principal parts the same.
7 *attentive* – the others are used only predicatively.
8 *apple* – it's the only countable noun.
9 *my* – it's a possessive adjective, the others are possesive pronouns.
10 *write* – past irregular.
11 *child* – plural irregular.
12 *natural* – the others all form negatives with -dis.
13 *shirts* – the others are all 'a pair of'.
14 *popular* – the others all form negatives with im-.
15 *news* – it's always singular.
16 *important* – the others are all negatives.

Activity 72

Find the odd word in each of the following. You will need to think about the pronunciation.

1 snowed, played, tried, waited, rained.
2 doubt, bout, bought, drought, out.
3 bow, row, cow, read, tear.
4 write, their, mail, case, bough.
5 knee, lamb, finger, palm, knowledge.
6 church, bus, pleasure, dish, praise.
7 chemistry, christian, chapel, machine.
8 review, repeat, rejoice, retail, resent.

Answers: *cut this off before you give it to the class.*

1 *waited* – -ed pronounced / ɪd /.
2 *bought* – doesn't rhyme.
3 *cow* – only one pronunciation.
4 *case* – no alternative spelling for word of same pronunciation.
5 *finger* – no silent letter.
6 *pleasure* – plural adds / z /.
7 *chapel* – only one with ch pronounced / tʃ /.
8 *retail* – pronunciation of re.

Activity 73

Three men went out to dinner. The bill was thirty dollars. Each man gave a ten dollar bill to the waiter. He took the bill to the office and they said there'd been a mistake. The bill should have been twenty-five dollars, not thirty. The waiter was supposed to give five dollars back to the men. He realised that five was difficult to divide by three, and the men did not really know how much the bill was anyway. So he kept two dollars himself and gave a dollar back to each man. That means each man had paid nine dollars and the waiter had two dollars, but 3 x 9 + 2=29, not 30. Where is the other dollar?

Activity 74

A woman drove her car one mile to the top of a mountain. Her speed was 20 km an hour. How fast must she drive one mile down the other side so that the average for the whole (two mile) journey is 40 km an hour?

Activity 75

A frog is at the bottom of a 30-metre well. Each hour it climbs three metres and slips back two. How many hours does it take for it to get out?

The fast train leaves A for B at exactly the same time as the slow train leaves B for A. The fast train travels at 100 km an hour, the slow train at 60 km an hour. Which train is further from A when they meet?

Two fathers and two sons leave town, but the population only goes down by three. How is that possible?

A clock strikes six in five seconds. How long does it take to strike twelve?

A man is looking at a picture; he says:
'Brothers and sisters have I none,
But this man's father is my father's son.'
Who is he looking at?

Activity 76 © W. Foulsham & Co. Ltd.

Can you solve the crime?

The Case of the Body in the Barn

You arrive at the large country home of wealthy Keith Kendall. Terry Ahern and Don Benning, the junior partners in Kendall's firm, lead you to the barn at the rear of the house. Inside, lying face up on the floor, is Kendall's corpse, with a kitchen knife sticking out of his chest.

You dust the handle of the knife and find one set of well-defined fingerprints. Then you take prints of Ahern and Benning, and compare them with the ones on the knife. 'The only prints on the knife are yours, Ahern,' you say. 'But you've told me the knife comes from the kitchen in the house and that you haven't been in the kitchen all day.'
'I can explain,' Ahern replies. 'Don and I drove here today on business. When we couldn't find Mr. Kendall in the house, we started looking for him. The estate is so large, Don and I separated. When I got to the barn, there was Mr Kendall, with that knife in him! I started to pull the knife out – that's how my fingerprints got on it – and that's just when Don came walking in.'

Don Benning says, 'You can imagine my horror when I walked into the barn and found Terry bent over the body – holding a knife! His face turned pale when he looked up and saw me.'
'It happened as I said!' shouts Ahern. 'I had no reason to...'
'How about that argument you had with him yesterday?' Benning says. 'You told me afterwards that you were fed up with his constant criticism, and you were going to do something drastic about it!'

'I didn't kill him,' Ahern mumbles. He turns to you. 'Could it have been suicide?' 'No it wasn't suicide', you say. 'It was murder, and I'm taking one of you with me for questioning!'

Whom do you suspect, and why?

Answer: *cut this off before you give it to the class.*

You suspect Don Benning because:
a) Only Ahern's fingerprints were on the knife, which leads you to believe he is innocent, and that someone wiped the handle clean after the murder and before Ahern touched it.
b) If it had been suicide, Kendall's prints would have been on the handle too.
c) If Ahern had done it, he would not have been so foolish as to wipe the handle clean and then deliberately incriminate himself by putting his prints back on the handle.

Activity 77

Work in pairs. Which of these holidays would you prefer to go on?

A week in England

Travel the human way by luxury coach and ultra-modern boat.

Dancing, casinos, cinema on board: just like an ocean liner. And then a week in real England. The Lake district, the best scenery in England. The nicest people. Staying at small hotels off the beaten track.

Tours arranged, but self-drive cars available. Hill-walking if that's what you like. Picturesque villages to wander around at your own speed.

Get away from the rush.
Anglo Tours

A week's trip to New York!

By fast, comfortable Jumbo jet. Charming stewards and stewardesses to calm your flying fears and pamper you all the way. All meals, wine, and in-flight cinema included.

Luxury Hotel

Foreign language guide available 24 hours a day. Guided tours every day. Your every need taken care of. Just say what you want and we do it.

That's our motto.
Americo Tours

Activity 78

Look at the timetable and advert. You are staying in Brighton. You plan to go to the Saturday matinee with a friend who lives in a London suburb. You'd like to have something to eat with the friend – either lunch before you go to the theatre, or something to eat afterwards. You don't want to get home after ten o'clock, though because you're expecting a phone call from your family. Discuss the arrangements with your friend.

Brighton – London
Mondays to Saturdays

	Brighton dep.	East Croydon arr.	Victoria arr.
SX	08.18	09.03	09.20
SX	08.35	09.22	09.39
SO	08.37	09.18	09.33
	09.00	09.52	10.08
SX	09.20	10.05	10.20
	09.37	10.18	10.33
	then at the following		
	minutes past each hour		
	00	52	08
	37	18	33
	until		
	16.00	16.52	17.11
	16.37	17.18	17.30
	17.00	17.52	18.11

SO – Saturdays only
SX – Saturdays excepted

London – Brighton
Mondays to Saturdays

	Victoria dep.	East Croydon dep.	Brighton arr.
	16.10	16.25	17.05
SX	16.30	16.47	17.36
SO	16.40	16.55	17.47
SX	16.55	17.10	17.57
SX	17.00	17.15	18.04
SO	17.10	17.25	18.05
SX	17.25	17.40	18.27
SX	17.30	17.45	18.35
SO	17.40	17.55	18.47
SX	17.55	18.10	18.57
SX	18.00	18.15	19.04
SO	18.10	18.25	19.05
	18.40	18.55	19.47
	then at the following		
	minutes past each hour		
	10	25	05
	40	55	47
	until		
	20.10	21.25	22.05
	21.40	21.55	22.51

THEATRE ROYAL
Tel: 405800
Mon – Thurs eve 8.00
Fri 5.30 and 8.45
Sat 3.00 and 8.00

Bubbling Brown Sugar

Now in its 2nd great year

Book by telephone for the entire family. Easy parking.

Activity 79

Complete each of these sentences. Don't just fill in the spaces quickly – think carefully about what you might want to say. Remember, you don't want to tell people everything about yourself!

I think I am … _____

_____

Other people say I am … _____

_____

By the time I am thirty I hope I will … _____

_____

Two of my favourite expressions are … _____

_____

The best advice my mother/father ever gave me was … _____

_____

My greatest secret is … _____

_____

Activity 80

Complete each of these sentences. Think carefully before you write.
Are you sure you want to tell the truth?

For me, money is very important/not very important because … ____

_____

For me, friends are … _____

_____

For me, pleasure is … _____

_____

For me, the most important thing about my country is … _____

_____

For me, the most important thing in life is … _____

_____

Chapter 14 Tried and tested ideas

Here are some more practical lesson ideas, drawn from hundreds sent in by former assistants. Decide for yourself which ones you could try with your level of classes.

Alibi

Last night there was a bank robbery. The police suspect two members of this class. The other members of the class act as interrogators of the two suspects.

a) Ask for two volunteers to act as the suspects. Give them an information sheet (prepared by you in advance) to help them construct their alibi. Send them outside the room to prepare.

b) Divide the rest of the class into two groups to construct questions to ask the suspects. Get them to make a list.

c) Bring the suspects in for the interrogation. This can be done with one suspect for each group, swapping, or in a smaller class in front of the whole class.

Love at first sight

a) Using the computer dating form on page 105 at a level suitable for your students. Number the forms. Ask students to write *M* (male) or *F* (female) at the top, then fill the forms in.

b) Collect the forms. Divide the class into pairs. Give out one *M* form and one *F* form to each pair.

c) Each pair must pretend they are that couple and write the story (or make notes) of their first meeting.

d) One from each pair reads out the story for the whole class.

Stuttgart to Salford, Avignon to Aberdeen

Students discover what language they would really need on a journey from their home town to the home town of the assistant.

a) Decide the different means of transport needed for the journey.

b) Divide the journey up into its different sections and brain-storm the language needed – for example: *to buy tickets, meals on train, get taxis, check-in desk.*

c) Gather all the language together. This could develop into a very useful project over several lessons.

Jumble sale

Bring in a collection of odd objects: complete works of Shakespeare, a kitchen object, item of clothing, some unusual food, something from your home etc.

a) Divide the class into pairs and give each pair an object.
b) The pairs decide the best way to 'sell' their object to the rest of the class.
c) The rest of the class can be run as an auction with each pair coming forward to try to sell their object to the whole class, or pairs can go round to each other trying to sell.

The interview

Find a very evocative picture of a person – a picture from which you can deduce a lot about the life of the person – for example, a tramp sitting on a pavement. Prepare an interview sheet with the interviewer's questions and blanks for the replies. Leave some space at the bottom for the students to make up some questions of their own.

a) Divide the class into pairs. Give the picture to one student and the interview sheet to the other. Give them a few minutes to prepare their part. (Weaker students should ask the questions.)
b) Ask some of the pairs to act out the interview in front of the whole class.

The island

Draw a map of an island on a sheet of paper, giving towns, rivers, roads, forests, beaches etc. On another sheet draw an outline map of the island with no features.

a) Divide the class into pairs. Give one student the blank map and the other the completed map.
b) Make sure they cannot see each other's papers – you could ask them to sit back-to-back.
c) The student with the detailed map then describes everything on the island while the other student fills their map in. (Be strict about them not looking.)
d) Students then compare maps.

Accent dictation

(Not for the faint-hearted!)

This is a simple variation on a dictation lesson. Find a suitable (fairly short) passage for dictation. The idea is that you read the dictation several times – each time with a different accent, for example, Scottish, American, Irish – if you can! Then finally, in BBC English. Then check that they have understood. You can finish this lesson with a discussion on accent in their own country: what is the 'best' accent? What do they think of other accents? What about some famous people in their country?

Picture dictation

(For younger classes)

Draw or find a simple picture, for example: country scene with mountains, stream, bridge, house, sheep, dog on bridge, tree, spotted cow, children under tree, clouds, rainbow etc.

a) Give each student a blank piece of paper. As you read and describe your picture, they have to draw it. Or, you could get different students to come out to the front and draw on the board.
b) Students then compare pictures.
c) Ask students to use the other side of their papers, folded in half.
d) Each student draws their own picture on one half of the sheet, then they work in pairs describing and drawing each others' picture. (Back-to-back is the best way to make sure they don't cheat!)

Simon says

(For younger classes)

The popular children's game, but prepared carefully.

a) Teach the parts of the body – get students to draw and label on the board.
b) Ask the class to stand, then play 'Simon says'. Here is a summary if you don't know: Teacher gives commands – for example, 'Put your hand on your head! Touch your left foot!' If the command is preceded by 'Simon says' students should do it. If you do not say 'Simon says' and a student obeys, they then have to sit down and drop out of the game. The last person left standing is the winner.

Old Macdonald

(for younger classes)

Whether you like it or not, thousands of former assistants have built hilarious lessons around the song 'Old Macdonald'! The typical lesson seems to have gone as follows:

a) Gather names of farmyard animals on board.
b) Ask students the noise each makes in their own language. Teach them the English noises – this can get out of hand – so keep control!
c) Give them the words of the song. Don't let this get too hilarious or you will make other teachers jealous of your obviously popular lessons!